UNCONVENTIONAL & *Spiritual Marriage*

Order this book online at www.trafford.com/07-1627
or email orders@trafford.com

Most Trafford titles are also available at major online book retailers.

Note for Librarians: A cataloguing record for this book is available from Library and Archives Canada at www.collectionscanada.ca/amicus/index-e.html

ISBN: 978-1-4251-4001-4

We at Trafford believe that it is the responsibility of us all, as both individuals and corporations, to make choices that are environmentally and socially sound. You, in turn, are supporting this responsible conduct each time you purchase a Trafford book, or make use of our publishing services. To find out how you are helping, please visit www.trafford.com/responsiblepublishing.html

Our mission is to efficiently provide the world's finest, most comprehensive book publishing service, enabling every author to experience success. To find out how to publish your book, your way, and have it available worldwide, visit us online at www.trafford.com/10510

www.trafford.com

North America & international
toll-free: 1 888 232 4444 (USA & Canada)
phone: 250 383 6864 ♦ fax: 250 383 6804
email: info@trafford.com

The United Kingdom & Europe
phone: +44 (0)1865 722 113 ♦ local rate: 0845 230 9601
facsimile: +44 (0)1865 722 868 ♦ email: info.uk@trafford.com

10 9 8 7 6 5 4 3 2

UNCONVENTIONAL & *Spiritual Marriage*

by Jeanette De Jonk

Authors' Introduction

I give gratitude to the infinite power that give me the creative energy, power and persistence to finish this book in order that someone else may find it useful. I thank and give gratitude to people who have loved me and who have helped me be who I am which is the direct result of what I've become today. I especially thank this mysterious spiritual love and creative power that emerged in me over night, the power that helped me get into the creative work I have only dreamed of so long, the mystical love that has left a mark in my heart forever for what ever that may be. I am grateful to the universe for letting me experience this magical love and to love and be loved. What a wonderful gift it is to feel the kind of pure love I feel in my heart. Nothing can replace this electricity that runs in my veins. I have no complins just gratitude that I feel so much peace, harmony, contentment and happiness for no apparent reason by just knowing my true self.

I started researching information for my own purposes to solve the problems and conflicts of myself, my life and my marriage. These are the problems that have been running in and out of my life for as long as I can remember. I wanted to finally get to the bottom of these problems and cut the branches that are poisoning my tree of life. This search for myself, truth and pure joy has opened a total new world of reaching to a higher level I never imagined. I am on a journey looking for answers and found the answers that help me find more tranquillity and balance in my life. Whether they are the answers I am looking for in the long run is not the issue but the fact that it brings me balance and awareness is what I appreciate about this journey I am travelling. I merely want to put forward the simple changes in life that brought me answers and happiness to better myself and be one with myself and in return to fall in love with me all over again. If I can help one person with my research and some principles I have followed I will be happy that my life's purpose to help others have been achieved to some extend. This book is yours to read, enjoy and take the facts the way you want and hopefully it will help you as much as it has helped me. Just remember when you open yourself up to changes; there are times when unexpected things will happen you will loose things you are not ready to loose and receive things and people that you never really asked for. The fact is when we open our self up to change the universe will give us what we are sub-consciously looking for or vibrations we are transmitting in order to make our self happy. Remember there are no co-incidents or accidents, everything happens for a reason and that is because we chose that way. Go with the flow and enjoy the ride and changes that come as there is a world out there that is waiting to give you the time of your life. Simply grab it before it slips you by. This is my healing journey which I would like to share with you. Thank you for enjoying this journey with me. I wish you all the very best in your own spiritual growth and journey and hope I will hear your story in the near future. Please write to me and share your stories with me. My e-mail address is jeanettedejonk@gmail.com

Contents

CHAPTER 1

What Is Marriage?

We all know the meaning of marriage in different terms or form. The meaning will differ from person to person. Marriage is a union between two individuals and the celebration of coming together as one. Marriage can be greatly influenced by our elders, parents, and teachers who had an influence in our childhood and even up until adulthood. From the time of birth someone's marriage has been a part of our life and we see more and more people getting married each year. Some might say that marriage is necessary to keep the family unity or marriage is to commit to one person for the rest of her life to show that person his commitment. Some might say, oh well it's just a piece of paper and I don't need that to show my commitment to my partner as he is the one I am spending my life with now and he might as well be my husband. People are content with various sorts of meanings about their marriage and at the end of the day what really matters is the commitments each other have in that relationship to love and to be loved no matter what form of living arrangement they choose.

My new found meaning of Marriage is a place where you can be yourself and has breathing space to grow personally and spiritually as and when I want without having to consult my partner about my changes. It is a beautiful place without suffocation, a place where you can learn and teach each other, a place where you do not feel prohibited and a place where you do not have to log in and log out. Marriage to me is to share my dreams and to help each other overcome them and to help each other in times of need and to not let them fall in times of trouble. Marriage is to expand your horizons and not to restrict them. Marriage is a total journey of trust, excitement, commitment and working towards one common goal. Marriage is a union that fills the gap of a person and marriage is continuos work to find peace, happiness and contentment. Marriage is ying and yang and a balanced life together. Marriage is a journey of expression to express your creativity, fantasies, inner most desires and most of all to experience and experiment them together in order to achieve harmony, contentment, and enlightenment together. Marriage is a journey of exploration of the mind, body and spirit. Marriage is to love totally and be loved with unconditions. Marriage is to gaze into each other's eyes and see your soul and know that you live with your one and only soul mate and that you are happy because you have found home at last. Marriage has become to me, where my dreams come true with this special other person to love and honour him in his times of need as well as mine. Love is the question and answer to all my problems, desires and wants because everything is solved with the simple act of love. In marriage I want to walk his and my life together and hold hands forever. This definition of marriage did not come to me over night it is a definition which I have learned with trial and error in my own life. I am thankful I finally feel I have an idea of what marriage is all about, if it happens to knock on my door one more time.

Some people put up and shut up and give their life into a miserable future in a marriage. This is not healthy for all who are connected with the marriage be it the couple, children and the external family. The ultimate problem lays in the couple who stick it out for all those years for the sake of the kids, money, time invested in each other, social, religious or family commitments, status or what ever their reason may be to hold that marriage together ignoring their own feelings for the external feelings and commitments. Then comes a time that we get all the freedom and the money we want to live comfortable but your heart is not comfortable because the dreams, goals and senses are lost and there is no vision for tomorrow. Marriage should never be an excuse, procrastination or a prison for your feelings or thoughts. Marriage should be an exploration to grow your soul to the ultimate climax and should be a wonderful journey from a caterpillar to a butterfly who will fly into freedom with beauty and self confidence. Marriage should not have any limits and should be a journey of trust in each other and trust that the journey will take its course. What ever any ones reason is, marriage is a very significant event in the society all around the world and it is a very personal experience to who ever gets into it. People hopefully found their soul mate and there is so much love to offer each other and they make a commitment to share their love and create that family that they always wanted.

A long anticipated dating game finishes with the decision to get married and claim each other forever in which point the lovers will start a journey as one. It is such a blissful time in our life when we get married and all is happy including the in laws, friends and children if there are any. Most of the problems that arise in this stage at this point are very minor issues compared to what's to come. Now the problems might be, in laws or the wedding ceremony etc. which are really nothing major to worry about. Usually even if problems arise in these areas it is pretty easy to brain storm and sort matters as we are so in love that we would do anything to compromise at this stage and have everything running smoothly. You simply do not want your love bubble busted. This is the fairy tale beginning of a very important part of all lovers life's and should be experienced and enjoyed to the fullest and hopefully marriage will only come once in a life time for many. But unfortunately or should I say fortunately this bliss is experienced 2 or even 3 times by more than 50% of our population. There are always advantages and disadvantages in everything in this world. So it applies to love and marriage as well. The disadvantage being all that hard work, emotional trauma, financial separations, grey hair and children will be greatly affected. On a positive note people who fall in love more than one time get lucky to feel and experience the high only falling in love will bring. The energy that the love experience gives us in the form of a super energy which connects to the supreme self. Lucky are those who had the advantage and took advantage of these energy without making the mistake of marrying over and over again but then there are a few of us who have a gullible heart and are simply silly romantics who believe love will follow with marriage and happily ever afters. The romantics dream shatters when the marriage finally ends up in the most un-expected ways. We are so blinded by love and our hearts are so full of love that we fail to see any early stage potential problems within two people. We should know that obviously when two people live together, they are two individuals and a matter of time when we will have problems of wanting our own needs met at any cost. Lot of people don't want to compromise. People can only show their good side for a small period of time in their relationship and then this ugly monster will emerge, the monster that we so desperately tried to hide from our partner all these months or years. Marriage is like a baby who needs lots of attention, nurturing and our time. If we are not capable of giving these three ingredients into the marriage, we really should not enter a marriage. Marriage is between two people who need to give close to equal time to each other, if one person gives all the time and the other doesn't in time the foundations of the marriage will crack and become a very bad habitual activity who live in a routine like robots. When we wake up every morning, we have a shower, put on our clothes, drink our coffee etc our partner should also be included in our day to day life. Take an interest in your partner and show him you care and he is loved. Don't take her for granted that she will always be there no matter what. Your partner is made out of flesh and blood and has very distinctive needs, wants and desires of her own and those needs must be met in order for her to feel fulfilled. If she feels her needs are ignored, you are guaranteed in the long run she will look to meet them some place else other than you and it will be a bit too late for you to work it out. She is not capable of been thrown in the back seat of your car to deal with at a later date. Obviously she cannot come first in your life every minute of your day but she should be given priority at any moment you can spare. Marriage is a union of constant work and progress and climbing the ladder as much as your career and may be even more. You cannot do a half job and get away at work, neither can you with your partner and if you think you can find short cuts you better adjust your mentality pretty quick or else your marriage will be adjusted before you know it. Take an interest, do little things that make her happy. A woman would love her husband calling her out of nowhere and telling her that she is important and that she is loved very much or that he has a surprise for her. You can arrange a bath for her or make a cup of coffee or make breakfast in bed or have a rose on her pillow when she wakes up first thing in the morning. These small gestures will take your wife's breath away and always have her love and loyalty more than up to your expectations. She will surprise you with her love, dedication, and respect for you and stand by you no matter what you go through in life. If you take her for granted, expect her to cook, clean the house, look after the kids, work and expect her to be your maid you my man is asking for trouble down the line. It may take one day, one year or 5 years but disaster is written in the fate of your marriage and is concluding faster than you would be happy about. I am talking in respect to both genders and is easier for me to talk my point of view and that is why it may sound like I am attacking men here but it is not the case. Please all men out there, who are reading, do not take this personally but where there is he simply replace it with her and you will benefit from the book too. Getting back to my writing, if you take your partner for granted it is the guaranteed recipe for a disastrous marriage. Take account for your actions from very early on and like you feed your body keep feeding your marriage because it is essential for your soul to keep your marriage happy and healthy. Our marriage becomes the reflection of the hard work we have invested all those years compacted into a happy or sad bundle.

We all want to get married. Even the most unconventional person would go ahead and get married so what is it about marriage that people go over and over again and just tie the knot. It is the same as when a mother has a baby, the pain she goes through she would sware that she would not have another child but as soon as she hold her child the pain is forgotten because the happiness is more greater than any pain she just experienced a while ago and in 1 or 2 years there she goes again at the second or third child and she has forgotten the past experiences totally. This is true also with love. We go through the roller coaster ride with love. We love and we hate and then we love again all because we humans are so addicted to those brain chemicals that we produce and we can't get enough of feeling the high points of being in love. It is simply magical and like being on an addictive drug which totally takes control of our emotions, body and mind and we just love it and allow it to happen over and over again. There is no room for a couple to take each other for granted in a marriage as half of our marriage is based on psychology, emotions attached to our partner and the way we look at him and feel about him. As you know you do not play with other people's emotions, it is very wrong and unethical. Love and marriage, has happened from the inception of time and it will happen until the end of time. The fact is that love and marriage will be an inevitable part of our lives just like birth and death. No matter what any one says or how much people write about love it is a journey that every individual will take differently in order to grow and learn as a person. At the end of the day how ever careful we are, when it comes to the matters of the heart we almost always dive in head first because we are simply blinded by love. We will therefore live, love and learn the hard lessons that love bring us and there is no changing this fact. The secret in the long run to a good relationship is to learn and know who we really are, what we want from life, accept and love yourself from within and be grateful for all the good things you have in your life and you will be closer to attracting the right partner to you and subsequently reduce the number of times you get hurt in the process of falling in love.

First things should be first and that is to know and love yourself unconditionally for who you are. It is best to have a very intimate relationship with yourself and get to know yourself in and out and make that a priority in your life. This way you are not a child anymore and you know exactly what you want from life and have broken some of your own bad habits that will attract in your relationships. Our desire to depend on someone else's love is so much greater that we instinctively give ourselves fully to a lover without testing our own waters and knowing what is it that we want from this relationship. To know oneself is the only answer to avoiding our ignorance and mistakes in life and it took me this long to learn that fact. Whether we like it or not we honestly cannot love someone unconditionally until we know how to love ourselves without restrictions. So let's start on a journey to love ourselves within first and in return to spread unconditional love around the world. When you are transformed through this kind of love, you will start to notice changes in your environment and true love will knock on your door. You will instantly feel and connect to this true love because you have not only being looking for this love but you know what this true love is, finally. This is the WOW moment you would have waited all your adult life and finally you can hold hands and step into the world to experiment and experience your life's purpose with this special someone. All good investments will bring its dividends and so will personal time invested in yourself. Wait, watch and know your signs of readiness and the universe will give your life's potential to have and to enjoy for a lifetime. If you have a marriage based on these rules of love, you truly are blessed in love and should cherish the union you have with your husband or wife.

CHAPTER 2

Where Happiness Comes From

Always try to captivate the positiveness we humans can feel such as being passionate, caring, loving, warm, smiling, confident, positive, cheerful, persistent, determined, curious, flexible etc. Happiness cannot come from anywhere else but from within you and believe strongly that you are happy and you will be happy. You can get traces of contributions towards happiness from others but happiness is a state of mind and is as simple as making up your mind and working very hard to maintaining that mind through persistence and faith. We can never be happy with anyone unless we are truly happy with ourselves. Happiness is born right deep inside our own self and you can never be happy unless you dig deep within you and find that happiness bug. Have a look at yourself and ask some questions. Am I happy, if not why, what makes me so unhappy, who makes me unhappy, why does this person make me unhappy, what do I contribute to that unhappiness, is there something missing in my life, should I do something different to make my life happy, am I happy with how I look, with my career, with my family, with my finances, with the way I live, have I found my souls purpose and most of all am I living with my Soul Mate right now and if not what changes should I make to have my Soul Mate in my life and many more questions that are significant to you. Write all your questions and write your answers and keep notes of your idea. Your answer will be more correct if you give attention to the first thing that come into your mind and not what you think is right because that is what you want to happen. Make one positive change every day or week does not matter how small it is, just matters that this small change is important to you. Surround yourself with positive people, books, tapes and everything that is positive. Every week type one positive affirmation and hang it in your bed room or bath room, where you will see often. Make one positive change every day or week and praise yourself for making that change. Make sure that these changes you are making are important to you not to someone else. This week you can hang a positive message and say "I am a go getter and where there is a will there is a way" next week you can say "positive attractions are my second nature and I attract everything positive to live my life" and so on. You can just make up your own positive affirmations that will suit your needs and every morning and night chant it and imagine that you are that person till you fall a sleep. Start chanting again when you wake up, in the car, while you are walking and while you are cooking and do not stop until you strongly believe this instruction in your brain and make it part of your subconscious thinking. Repeat the words a thousand times if you must until you start believing what you are saying and until you can feel these words inside your body mingling with every cell in your body. Discard all negatives you feed into your brain and life. If there are negative people around you tell them you do not wish to listen to their negatives and if they don't listen distance them temporarily until your brain is strong enough to handle these situations. Surround your self with mentally powerful people and get good strong friendships going. Really focus and give value to your thoughts and look for clues to success in your life and have faith in the infinite power and be grateful. We all have been told knowledge is power and time is money so use these to your advantage. Validate your new idea with love and desire so the law of attraction will bring this element to you. Quality of our thoughts will be the result of our experiences in life. The more energy we radiate the more positive thoughts and actions we can produce. One smile will attract thousands of smiles and this concept is the same to anything else in your life. Always keep your mind healthy and full of happy attitude. Brain storm all negatives in your life to positives and change one bad habit every week to one positive habit. When you feel negative, feel with intensity of an event that was happy in your life and energise yourself with those happy vibrations. Life is what you make of it and the thoughts you think and the meanings you give them is how life will be for you. We are here to grow as individuals and if we stop growing we are as good as dead. When you decide to change don't think about what others will say about your changes because almost always most people will not like those changes because you our out of their comfort zone and it is too much for them to handle. You go after the changes you want, even if you had to make the same mistake a thousand times it never is too late to make the changes in your life but the key is to use the power within you now and make these changes right now. You can only control the present moment and give all you have to the present moment and do something good for yourself. We do not want to feel dead, we want to be and feel alive while we are still kicking. Talk is cheap so stop story telling and procrastinating and do something for your life as actions are what make us into something. Learn the art of only speaking what you mean and keep notes of it if you must and try and keep promises to yourself to do what you said you would. To be true and reliable to yourself is very important in the process of learning to trust yourself and do not fail yourself. Make every attempt to keep to your promises and goals and if you cannot, re-evaluate and make necessary changes to your goals and give it an estimated arrival date which is realistic to you.

I remember before I had our son Bradleigh, I wanted a child so badly and that is all I dreamed and thought about. This was my obsession at the time so I went through so many magazines and collected pictures of everything about pregnancy starting from the journey of the sperm and egg, their love dance which forms into an embryo. The baby growing in the mothers womb at first, second and third trimester and finally the baby born and suckling at his mothers breast. I made a chart with these pictures in the above order and I looked at these pictures and memorised them in my brain and I told myself over and over that this is the life that will take form inside my body soon. I stuck it on the fridge and looked and memorised these picture in my head to create them into a memory so I can send it to my brain as what I want to happen next in my life. I repeated that I was pregnant with a boy so beautiful, healthy, spiritual and talented. After we tried for the baby I pictured the life form the way it was on the picture and imagined that the egg and the sperm will have their love dance and then fertilise and walk hand in hand through the fallopian tube into my uterus where it will form into a healthy embryo. I believed that this is what was happening inside my body. When this did not happen the first month the way I imagined I was upset but I told myself that my belief should be more strongly focused next month but with even stronger desires and feelings and I achieved my desired results and was so overjoyed. With our second son I did not need pictures as I was very connected to the vibrations and sensations of my body. I could almost picture what is happening inside my body so after we tried to have Jarrod, I touched my stomach and meditated and spoke out while holding my stomach what was happening inside my stomach. I imagined and pictured what was happening inside my body and everyday I would talk to myself and say what was happening that day inside my body. After a week of conception I strongly believed I was pregnant and my husband did not think I would be pregnant in the first month because I was still breastfeeding our son Bradleigh. I did a pregnancy test at ten days and to my disappointment it showed negative but I still insisted on believing that I felt the sensations of having a baby grow inside my body and nothing was going to change that fact until I got my period. In another week I did not get my period and did another pregnancy test and I found I was pregnant and my husband was so surprised that I could breastfeed and get pregnant in the first attempt. I truly believed that my strong desire to get pregnant and all my energy focused on this one concept got me the kids I wanted and we can do this with absolutely anything. I always got critised for being a dreamer as a child but I have finally learned to dream again like a child and an inventor and it feels wonderful and natural. The biggest winners are those who have the desire and faith to win and achieve their victories and the failures are those who quit prematurely due to lack of faith. So never quit always perceiver until you see your results in front of your nose. Be the captain of your ship and navigate it to any destination you so desire as there are no limitations in where you can go it is totally up to your imagination. Make your desires and dreams your obsession and obsess every minute until you have it in your hand and until you feel the benefits of your hard work. Give back to the world of yourself and the world will give back to you. You cannot receive until you give willingly and be open to receive what the universe want you to have.

Also when I was pregnant with our son Bradleigh I strongly believed that I will have a one hour labour, from the minute I thought about labour. I believed it so strong and only connected the process of labour with one hour and finally when the day did come for delivery of our son I had a one hour labour out of which 15 minutes were second stage labour. With our son Jarrod I believed I will have also a one hour labour but had a 1 ½ hour labour out of which second stage labour was 1 minute and the rest of the labour was not very stressful and painful as Bradleigh's birth. With our son Jarrod I was not dilating as I should and the mid wife said I might take longer than our first son for the delivery and that did not sit well in my mind. I told myself that is not going to happen if I have something to say about that. I just got this brain rush where it is not going to be hours for me to have this baby and it is going to happen now. I wanted to get up and go have a hot shower and sit down on a birthing chair because that was my first gut feeling. The mid wife helped me get to the shower. I got there and parked myself on the birthing chair and it only took one minute from the very second I sat on that chair, I just gave one mighty scream and there I was with our second son out in this world within one minute. I never had to push for the boys to be born, they came naturally so it was not like I really tried to push the kids out. My mind was so focused on what I wanted that nothing could stop having these kids out safely and quickly. I thanked my sub-conscious mind for standing by me and being my strength because that is exactly what happened. These are just classic examples of putting our desires with faith to work.

I just give you these examples not to gloat about my experiences but to show you how positive they are and how powerful these emotions were and how positive affirmations and emotions can get the results you want. When no one else did, I was totally focused and believed in what I must do and focused all my energy I had in my body in delivering this baby FAST and safe and nothing would stop me at that point. We can all focus and have faith in what we want and do this, just do not let any one get in your way of your belief. Anything you put your mind to do is possible as long as you totally believe and have faith in your own higher power. The very moment you visualise your desires, and make up your mind your future events begin to unfold and circumstances you need for your new believes will unfold. With belief and faith your dreams will come true. All our thoughts, actions and deeds leave an impression on us and create the road to our future. Good and positive thoughts will create simply good and positive circumstances and future. Plant a seed and visualise what you want to happen and affirm every day and every hour. If you imagine it is possible to have what is in your dreams then it is possible to have these desires in real life as your imagination is the greatest of assets. Always visualize the events, circumstance and spiritual path you would like to take and visualize that they have come to realisation in your present state and feel the pleasure of these enjoyments and the tantalizing feelings they bring. Don't be afraid to be the inventor and the creator of your own thoughts and thereby your future, do it because you want it that bad and because there is a purpose and passion to what you are doing. Our life path is our choice so choose to be what you want to be. Everything you do should be injected with intense emotions and feelings and should be your total focus of what you truly want in your life. Naively just believe in that path you want or the things you want and don't worry about how you get there, it doesn't pay to try to be too smart sometimes. Believe like a child who believes in her vision no matter what adults say. The more you want something in life, the more positive vibes you would give to these thoughts and put enormous amount of feelings to make it real and as if you have it in your possession NOW. What you see, imagine and dream will become real, and what you dream comes true. Don't go after what you want out of anger, fear or competition. Go after your dream because you have such an intense desire to have this dream so bad that you can't live without it. Everyday put intense emotions to make this dream a reality until you actually gravitate towards owning up and living your dream. If you see it in your visualisation and feel then it is a matter of time before it is a reality and in your possession. Our thoughts are our cause and experiences are the effect. All thought is received by the brain according to our reasoning. Meditate and give intense vibrations to make these dreams alive and strongly believe and make them apart of your sub-conscious in order that the sub-conscious mind will not reject the thought and accept as your actual dream and work on attracting what you want. Go on doing good, thinking good thoughts continuously and you will soon do and think good. Most people live in fear that they will loose their job, their partner, their possessions etc and they eventually attract what they fear because they give meaning and power to their fearful thoughts. Why not give meaning to what you love the most and give meaning to what you want with passion. Don't give your power away unnecessarily give your power only to the most meaningful and most wanted things in your life. The most wise choice for us in life is to keep moving forward to the light and to do what you want even if it is to the unknown and leave the fear behind with all the negatives that our attached to it. Always be grateful to all that you have in your life and never pass a day without sending your humble gratitude to the universe. Be thankful and grateful for all the good things you have in your life. Remember you honestly get and attract what you want, so if you wish evil or send negatives to someone else you are sure to get them knocking on your door sometime soon. Just work with the positive and leave the negative behind. Remember only do to others what you would like others do to you. You would not like others wishing you bad or doing bad things to you, so don't do this to others either. Plant the seed of love and see how it grows into a beautiful healthy tree. Learn to give and take and to go with the flow. One of the best advises that anyone has given me is to go with the flow. When this friend gave me these words of wisdom, I thought to myself "yes, that sounds logical and what is there to loose, may be that is the way I should learn to live, just go with the flow". Little did I know how much these words would change my life and these words have become like gospel to me because they are so powerful and have opened doors in every direction of my life.

You must learn to love yourself, and give attention to yourself before you learn to love others. You can only learn giving by giving and no other way. Help yourself from the highest form of mental attitude because this is the tool you need to be happy in life. If you have a strong mind and you have found happiness you will live happy and allow other people to make you happy. Use all the life's ups and downs as circumstances for life lessons which take you to higher levels. The universe never gives you any situations unless they are needed for your growth and these circumstances are what you attracted with your own thinking pattern to help you grow as a person and take you to a higher dimension.

Write down and make a plan for what you want from your life. Divide your big goals and dreams into small achievable goals and divide into small time frames such as I will achieve this in one month, three months or one year and give a completion date to those goals. Don't float around life with unclear goals and make your life and yourself complicated. I did this most of my life and never want to go back again because all it does is make one mistakes and make another mistake to cover up my previous mistakes. My goal was to help my partner achieve his goals and I just ignored myself in the process. When your partner does not achieve his goals because he is stuck in his own world eventually you are stuck too and the answer to this is to have your own achievable goals and name them yours to achieve. Don't make life into a bowl of excuses and because you are a woman does not mean you have to live by your husbands dreams. We are all entitled to have and achieve are own individual goals and that is our birth right. You can only achieve when you have a desire and get focused on what you want. If you have a strong will, give it a go and back up your will with a strong faith then there is nothing impossible for you to achieve or overcome. We are made of what we think and feel so get the guidance of your higher self through meditation to make you a strong and focused individual. Make it your mission to accomplish all your desires and be happy. We are in this world to learn as much as we can and to experience life to its fullest potential and in the process find the ultimate happiness.

CHAPTER 3

Love, Desire And Sexual Energy

Sexual energy would work in par with spiritual energy. Both these energies are supernatural energies which have profound effects on the human brain. The sexual energy is released through unconditional love, sex and desire. When we harness these vibrations and power into our own formula to convert our creative talents into something magical, we truly did pull out the genius in us out into the world. This sexual energy can be converted to making our dreams come true which in return will bring happiness into our life in all forms.

Sex is the most powerful desire a human can have and when motivated by sex we can be so strong willed, imaginative, courageous, go getters, persistent and extremely creative and can open up creativity in arts, writing and drama. It is important that people learn to put these desires into very useful practices otherwise that energy can be wasted and be of no use to yourself or the world.

If someone can shift the sexual energy into some creative project, that person truly is very lucky as she has used the sexual power to tap into the genius in her and flourish this into something magical. People have always used the sexual energy into creating beautiful art, music and songs. We have always heard people say that their driving force for any artistic talents were the love they have for a woman or man in their lives. When driven by the sexual desire, romance and true love we can get super charged to achieve what ever we focus this energy on and this new found motivation will drive us to achieve absolute wonders and more than our hearts desires. The obsession we have with this sexual desire and love should be converted to energy that can tap into our genius powers to create because we all have it stored in our brain. These sexual desires sends the human brain on a crazy ride and stimulates the brain to the extend that it feels like a person is on a drug and these brain waves of love will take this person to a high frequency plane which is out of the ordinary. Our minds at this stage is so open to everything that we will find ways to communicate with the universe and these unknown forces through any vibrations that are open to us in order to experience these energies in the new found creative forms. This can also be called as if we are tapped into our sixth sense. When people are in this sixth sense state or they have a gut feeling or their higher power talks to them it is like an inner voice whispering ideas or your course of action to be taken. We should never be ignorant to this inner voice who gives us messages as our sub conscious mind knows what we want much better than we do. So never ignore your gut feelings and this little voice that talks to you. Stop to take note of this little person with so much wisdom and take time to be silent and really listen to your inner child.

People in today's day and age are so driven by the temporary sexual desire that has only physical pleasure for the moment. I don't believe most even have an idea of the spiritual awakening or benefits they can acquire via the proper combination of a suitable partner in a metaphysical level along with the feelings of romance, desire and love. People abuse this power switching from one partner to another and giving very little regards to what messages and healing the sexual drive can bring into any ones life. How great the world would be if we learn to focus this energy to something more bigger than us. The sexual desire and spiritual urges are very closely connected. When someone is totally in love with another person and when you know this is the person you have waited all your life it is like a spiritual connection happens instantly and you feel a sense of calmness and balance like you have never experienced before. In this state of pure love, you can never compromise your life ever again and will always search like a child for the pure and the simplicity of everything you come into contact. If you connect with this special person, with this special love that gives you the power, consider yourself very lucky because it does not come everyday of your life, for most it may come once a life time. This kind of love is not about physical connection and the physical pleasure that we experience. It is about the world that opens to the unknown, the buttons that press in our sub-conscious mind, the creativity that flows and breads through our whole body, mental satisfaction, how you look into your own eyes and see yourself with love and respect for yourself you never experienced before, the love that you feel and the love that runs in your blood like a magical power to cleanse you into the pure and lovable person who want to love with un-conditions and without expectation because you have a burning fire inside your heart that burns with hunger to love and to be loved.

Try and utilize these creative forces and meditate while you connect with your partner to guide you to the highest level the universe can take you. Close your eyes and plant the seeds you need for your future because this is indeed a very magical moment. Talk to your partner about a meditation process to heal both yourselves while connecting with each other, in order that you may use this supreme power for the better of both yourselves and maybe even the world.

Imagine with faith that you possess this dream that you so badly want as if you have it now and put all your emotions and make this dream a reality and hold the picture in your head. When this picture is so real the sub-conscious mind will help bring this picture into reality and attract all circumstances to make this dream real. Go with the flow and put these circumstances into action and give it all you have and keep focused in your ultimate plan and what you should achieve. Never give up and never validate these dreams with negatives and only feed as much positives as you can every single day. Nurture it like a baby and it will flourish into something magical than you ever dreamed of. If your dream does not come true, believe more strongly and don't give up just pick yourself up and follow the procedure once again with more persistence and faith and you will get it right as soon as you get your mental conditioning right. Just remember the mind is a creature of habit and will absorb everything positive and negatives that you feed your mind. So your aim should be to nourish your brain with all positive and totally ban negatives.

Love, romance and sexual desires are the most powerful human emotions that exist and anyone in love can be noticed straight away with the sparks in her eyes. Don't be obsessed with keeping love forever; just enjoy love when it comes even if it is for a day, month or a year. What this true love teaches does not ever leave our soul, it always leaves positive traces for ever and it makes our life and us more beautiful and meaningful. So why worry about tomorrow when love has knocked on the door today and you are locked behind the door with your lover. Do not try too hard to control your new found love because love needs breathing space, freedom and room to grow. If you really love someone just let them free and enjoy each moment that is given to you and you will see that love will last forever but if you suffocate that love you will find it gone one day to never come back. If you love someone and they don't respond to you the way you would prefer them to and if you really know that they love you, don't give up too soon to get rid of your love because you did not get things your way. Just be with your lover with patience so he can come around, push yourself to move forward and show him love with persistence and open your heart to love him and communicate with him and this persistence will bring your lover to his home sooner than you think. When in times of trouble or hard times think back to a time when you were in love and the happiest memory you can think of and see how fast your problems will disappear and the memories will take you to a fantasy world where you get lost and never want to come back. Love comes when love wants to come without any guarantees or expectations and if we welcome the possibilities of opening ourselves to this miracle in life we will have a ball of our lives. The true love is never ever lost entirely; it will always keep imprints of that person's soul on your soul. What you do with this love and how you deal with it is how it will effect where your love will go. Love is a very spiritual gift, so use that gift to make yourself and your lover get closer together and to achieve something magical and higher than life can normally give you. This will be the biggest and best experience you will ever have in your life time and the closest you will reach to infinite intelligence. If marriage is not blesses with this kind of love and desire, no matter how hard or how much you try, there will be a time when your soul will realise that your soul is lost without this much needed closeness to this special somebody. Our souls are here to experiences the ultimate happiness and anyone spiritually connected will never settle for second best and will sooner or later run after what is her birth right which is to find her soul mate, to love him with true love, romance and to experience the ultimate desires of sexual energy. Sexual contact, pleasure and desires are as important to us as food, water and the air we breathe. Love, romance and desires are what is necessary to hit the right spots to get those creative juices flowing. What kind of life would we live without the essence of true love and the experiences these spiritual bliss brings into our lives? Without finding true love with our soul mate eventually our soul will loose sight of the meaning of life and thereby bringing misery into our lives which we fight a life time to resolve. By living with our soul mate we connect and live more simply without even trying too hard as the soul mate's main purpose is to make each other happy and content.

CHAPTER 4

When Children Are Involved

Remember that when a marriage comes to an unhappy place it almost always stays that way and it is only a very small percentage of the time it will change to a better place. Every one wants to assume that an unhappy marriage problem can be turned to a sweet marriage by just snapping your fingers. It really isn't this simple as it takes a lot of wrong and unfair doing from the couple's part to get to this unhealthy marital state. We can't pretend that everything is OK for a very long time. Sooner or later the elastic won't stretch far enough and it will snap and when that happens, reality just hits in your head and we start to wake up and smell the coffee. We unfortunately assume that we have been in the marriage for so long, now we have kids and we should stay together for the sake of the kids, money, status, power or what ever the couple's personal reasons are. I can assure you that these needs aren't going to keep your marriage together for long and you definitely won't keep the kids happy for too long either. Children will one day grow up and see that their parent's marriage is a very ugly marriage and will smell the problems in the family. Our children sensed problems even at their age especially our 3 year old son. You don't want to give children the idea that an unhealthy marriage is the key to a married life. Either fix it and be happy in your marriage or let each other go and be happy and respectful to each other outside your marriage. If our children see problems in the marriage all the time and see the parents together for life, they will one day grow up and attract the same kind of trouble in their own relationships. They will go on to living marital problems just as their parents and assume everything is perfect and the marriage is healthy. Children are not the cause of any marital problems and children never contributed to the marriage crises. The external factors such as poor communications, third party influences, financial problems, career problems, physiological problems, lack of support from each other etc that has contributed to the marriage crises at hand. People make the mistake everyday that if they stay in the marriage things will work out over time. In fact if you do stay in the marriage you will loose your real identity and loose all your motivation in life. You learn to be less aggressive and get into bad, unhealthy and unmotivated "what ever mood". It is a healthy state to have a bit of an aggressive spirit to go after what you want and to get it and you don't want to loose that in a hurry. A relationship will always have its ups and downs and love alone won't sustain a relationship. The person you fell in love is a different person in 10 years as we all change as time goes by. If you keep going with a bad relationship it will affect the children even more. You should either sort out the relationship or end it before you get kids to believe that marriage is an illusion. You will be surprised to see how many kids will understand if you sit and talk to them about how the marriage and why it is not working. Children just need to know that they can still have their mother and father both around them and they will still be loved the same way. Children will find ways to adapt and respect the parent's decisions. Instead of worrying and feeling miserable learn to utilize your time wisely to spend with the kids, do the things you never did, spend with friends or go and see new places and take up those hobbies you always wanted to do. Don't just sit at home and ponder on that miserable marriage. There is no perfect man or woman and definitely no perfect marriage we need to work on these issues. But when you do marry your soul mate it does get a lot easier as the two would talk and try to make things happen as their common interest is each other. Ask your sub conscious to guide to the truth and the changes needed in the marriage. I believe staying together for the kids is a big mistake for both of you as well as for the kids. Living with a man you don't love is one of the biggest mistakes of your marriage and kids will learn that a marriage is something that kills the love eventually and this is the ultimate result of marriage. A divorce is better than you teach your kids that disfunctional relationships are normal and they grow up and end up in the same boat. They won't know what a caring and loving relationship is because that is not what they grew up with. They will grow up and find a non-caring and non-loving partner just as they saw in their parent's relationship to each other. Emotional security is the best thing to give the children if parents are living in a loving and respectable marriage, other wise it is a pointless exercise to hold on to something you don't have. Spend at least 10 minutes of your busy time with each child just before bed time just talking to each child about your day and just connecting with the child without expecting anything in return from him. He will soon realise that this is a normal thing where my parents connect with me and they have no demands from me. He will eventually open up to the parents as well and talk about himself. Learn to listen to your children and what they are saying to you and try and understand the child's point of view and try to come up with helpful solutions to the problems. Try and avoid the words No or Wrong and say you are almost there because you don't want your child to give up so easy. Give your children the confidence that they are good at what they are doing. Don't just nag children about their bad habits always try to see and remember the good your child do and try and praise him for those good deeds? Try to acknowledge the child's reality how ever stupid it may feel. Play, read and spend time with your kids and show them you can be as much fun as kids and be consistent in everything you do. These are stronger and reliable security measures to take than to pretend to play happy house and family for the sake of the children.

CHAPTER 5

Are You Codependent

We really do not realise when we are dependent on a person as it only gradually builds up with the relationship over time. We depend on someone so totally because we do have some problem which is not resolved deep within ourselves. We have to try and find what that problem is. Would fear be the cause of your dependency? May be you are so fearful of facing life without a partner, or loosing material wealth, fear of being criticized by others, fear of losing your love, fear of dying alone, fear of getting sick and not having someone to look after you, fear of your past and past mistakes. Fear is a sign of weakness. Fear should be discarded from you before any positive results are shown as fear is the darkness of our soul who stops everything moving forward. Fear has been the primary controlling factor of the human race from inception of time. We are controlled by religion, culture, parents, teachers, partners, children etc on a day to day basis. In our society fear is the driving force to control someone else. Most of our adult life we try to overcome the fear that our parents, religion, culture or some other significant person planted in our head when we were young. Most parents spend all their energy creating fear in their children most of their childhood years in order to bring structure and order that they believe is necessary. This leaves us with the burden of fighting to overcome the fear that parents implanted in our head most of our adult life. Fear comes from feeling powerless and no connection to the higher power. Our parents did not know any better because they were never thought any different. However we now have the choice to choose not to live in fear and not to pass this fear factor into our children's lives. This practice will ensure in a few generations that the most negative emotion is discarded to the best we can from our society. We all need to dedicate ourselves to overcome the battle of fear. We can ask guidance from our high conscious. Go into silence and confront your fear. Lack of searching for who we really are will bring un-fulfilment in the long run. Just search for your own answers that make sense to you. What ever hold us dependent must be analysed and this habit must be broken in order to release ourself and our soul from this unhealthy emotion. I was fearful of my past and the vicious cycle that may continue again and again. I did not want to do the same mistakes I did in the past or the mistakes my mother did but never really did anything to change my mistakes either. I did not forgive my mistakes and accept me for who I was because I was too comfortable where I was and wanted to be stuck there and not change. I complained nagged, procrastinated, made excuses and blamed everyone but myself for the predicament I was in. I should have invested time into sorting all my negatives and change and seek guidance to see the light at the end of the tunnel. It is such an essential part of problem solving to sort out your childhood and circumstantial fears before you step into the future. I have always been dependent on someone else to smother me with love and had to learn to take responsibility for my own self and love me for who I am until I did that no one can love me the way I really want to be loved. I will only attract my mirror image of who I am. So I found the courage to not be depended on others and depend and trust my own instincts and gut feelings. When I made decisions I used to always go with what others thought was good for me and neglect what I thought but now even if others do not agree and I have a gut feeling to do something I will just do it. I realised that at the end of the day I have to know and have faith that I am doing what is best for me. No one else will know better about me than my sub conscious mind so it became imperative that I learn to listen to my inner voice and take note of what is been told within me.

First of all ask yourself are you co-dependent and if yes why are you so dependent on this person or relationship. May be someone told you that you cannot have a relationship or there is something wrong with you and ask yourself who said that. Your parents', relative, ex boy friend or husband. We end up being dependent on people or things for so many reasons that sometimes we ourselves cannot understand. It is not always bad but most times it cannot be healthy to depend on something or someone so totally. The primary person to depend on is your own self. It is best to look within to get your answers and strength.

With true love there should only be a reaction of bliss. Real love makes us unattached not dependent. Where there is real love, it does not rest on physical attachment at all. Real love will survive even if the lovers are a thousand miles away from each other. When you love someone totally and without attachment, your love will be so strong and never die and have a very strong foundation. True Love never produce any painful reaction, pain only comes through attachment and expectations. If your relationship is making you sad, and think things will get better over time, think your partner will change; you really are trying to cope with a difficult relationship which is not moving forward into a healthy region. We have to always remember that we cannot change others, we can only change ourselves. Ask yourself if your relationship started on a positive note or as a rebound. These situations necessarily may not be co-dependency but just an unhealthy relationship. These situations can be difficult to change but with focus and determination you can get into a healthy relationship over time. Sometimes when the dependency is sorted out which was what held the relationship together, there may not be a relationship left at the end of the healing process or may be other emotions and factors came into the picture such as jealousy, possessiveness etc. If these other emotional factors come in to the relationship, then they will need to be sorted out in the same process. If the co-dependency is stopping and hindering your growth there is no other alternative than to move on and free your partner and yourself. Let nature take its course and what is meant to be will be. What you find the most fearful are the very changes you need to change in order to grow up. Take the step and don't look back. Imagine your life as if it has already happened and as if you have that in your possession and create a possible and realistic world in your subconscious mind or the subconscious mind has nothing to work with. Let only the positives into your life and leave the negative behind. If someone is a hindrance to your growth leave them behind temporarily until you are emotionally fit to embrace the changes you need. Dealing with dependency is difficult enough for any one and you have to work hard to over come it. It is important to know what is right and wrong and take proper measure to make it alright and sort out your inner most feelings and addictions. You have lived with dependency for a long time now and must learn a different way of living and the best way to do it is to learn the art of learning to satisfy yourself. Habit is second nature and everything is the result of habit. Most of our daily problems and anxieties come from not being able to control our will power and mind. Buddha said "We are what we think, all that we are arises with our thoughts, with our thoughts we make our world" and how true is that as only we have the power to control what goes on in our mind unless offcourse you give that power away to someone else to control your mind. We are the commander of our own ship and the master of our own destiny so why be the commander and the master if we don't take control of our own lives. Learn to listen to your gut feelings and go with the flow. Sometimes we rather take the easy way out and ignore what our subconscious mind is talking to us about. When we sit in silence to meditate and really listen to what our mind, body and spirit is trying to tell us, take note of these messages because the subconscious mind is trying to talk to us of what our future direction should be. When you ask for a question from your subconscious mind, listen very carefully to the first word or words that come to mind or pay attention to the picture information that you get in your brain or co-incidental factors you attract in your life because all these things might be giving very helpful answers if you care to listen.

We depend on so many factors of life such as our partner, our fear, our past, our beliefs, what others may think and suppress our true feelings. These suppressed feelings will act out in our body and be felt in our muscle and slowly the blood circulation and then the energy in our body will be blocked. We eventually stop feeling ourselves and get stuck what we call "stuck in a rut". This really is a sad place for any person to be as it looses the true meaning of why we are here and the true meaning of our purpose and life. We have to open our nervous system to feel, our hearts to feel love and our sub conscious mind to rule in order for us to feel our wisdom. Being out of touch with ourselves is to be out of touch with other people and the world around us, the universe and our higher guidance. If we are being controlled by some other person or emotion or ego then it is time now to break free of these bad habits and set ourselves open to embrace more bigger and better habits. We must learn to let go of those long accumulated negative emotions and tension. We have learned to feel and express our emotions inappropriately. We have to learn to be happy and feel good of ourselves and radiate positive feelings around us. We have to learn to live in the here and now and make the most of this precious gift called "Our life". Let life take its natural path and do not hold things or people for the sake of your collection, you have to let go of people you are holding and give in to the natural laws of the universe and have faith that you have given up what is no longer necessary and the universe now will give you what you are looking for and what is necessary for you to be happy.

Good habits come with practice and practice come with repetition. We all have the need to express and that becomes our spiritual goal. Repetition is the key to create good habit in our brain. If we have a routine and do the same things everyday the same way as we do to create routines for our children we will also start getting patters that last in our brain. In order to embrace any attitude or habit we have to stimulate our brain with practice and repetition on a regular basis and it will become your inner most desirable habit. If you want something repeat this desire in words and actions over and over again until you reach your desired goal. Repetition will tell your subconscious of the expected outcome and eventually our brain will embrace the changes but it must be repeated and reminded over and over again until it is an accepted fact. Meditate and do yoga for higher help. Let go of all unwanted things in your life. Let go of people who do not serve a purpose anymore because may be your karmic debt is paid off with this person in this life time. Let nature take its course and let go of the old to welcome the new which is abundant and necessary for your growth. Live and learn at the present moment and let go to make room for what must be. Life will be blissful and abundant and you will thrive with your life purposes. The possibilities are endless and the opportunities are out there, we just need the realisation. The realisation cannot come to us unless we let go of everything we are being held and start to think independently for your own self and start claiming what ever that is that you dream. Let go of your dependencies and claim your power back in your own hand and manipulate it to achieve what you've come to do in this life time. Achieving your life purposes is better done now than later. Please leave this book now and have a closer look at all your desires, hopes, wants, achievements and goals and how you can achieve them and in what time frame. Give yourself a dead line to achieve these goals. Only write those goals that suit you and are for the improvement of yourself. Ask yourself why you need these goals and what achievements or happiness will come out of them. Revise your goals regularly and keep up with your demand. Never ever give up, until you have achieved what you want and that should be your biggest goal in life.

CHAPTER 6

Is My Marriage "Save Proof"?

When we are married and have children every step should be considered to get the help needed in order to save ourselves and our marriage, if the marriage can be saved. Major sacrifices must be made to force those changes. Most of us fall in love with our so called soul mate, the special somebody, the universal love mate, the partner we intend to live the rest of our lives with. When changes take place in our lives such as getting married, having a child, loosing a job the real personality come to light and we find how love can eventually change from a gain to a loss. When changes are not taking place in appropriate ways or when the love is going through a slow death we can totally loss faith in our marriage and this can change the dynamics of our family, relationship and feelings. What ever is said and done, we can choose how we feel in the long run and how we choose to continue to love and commit to our partner. If you are feeling let down or unable to re-connect with your partner, try and understand why you feel the way you do and how you got to that place in order to get a perspective of what you are going through. This is not necessarily the answer to solving the relationship problem or the crises but it may open your mind to your inner most desires and what you expect from yourself and your partner. Eventually our sub-conscious mind is designed to meet the needs of our inner most desires and will fight to get to a climax in what we believe. No one can tell us how to feel, what to do and where to go and only we will know the answers to these questions. We can be stuck in fear of the unknown and guilt of hurting our partner until such time when we make a total commitment to ourself and our soul to do right by us. We will go one step forward and two steps back until we learn to make up our own mind and stand by it and not get distracted by external factors and material things which stop your spiritual journey. As marriage progress every year things don't stay the same, people change, circumstances change and the man and woman in the relationship change and we must learn to make adjustments to these changes in order to make room for the new. It always isn't easy but in order to nourish a marriage people have to learn to adapt or accept responsibilities for cracks that may form in the marriage foundation. We must change with the changing world and our changing partner in order to live in a healthy now. Mostly learn to change with your changing partner, love and support her and you are doing the first thing right in your responsibilities towards your marriage. What happens when one partner changes and the other doesn't is that she would experience life in a different light and she will not get the fulfilment she wants from her partner. Both their priorities change with time and both pull towards the opposite direction in order to meet their own needs. She starts to know and accept herself as she likes this new found "love me" attitude and she would want to grow more of her inner personality. She finds her new found confidence and this puts her in a "high, happy go lucky" situation. She finds in herself the unconditional love, acceptance, respect, importance, recognition, sense of belongingness and this burning desire for the truth in what she wants in her life. Her inner child comes out and she becomes more playful and open to new ways of living and starts to live out of her comfort zone. She starts to grow and blossom from a bud to a beautiful rose that radiates. Her knew found growth recharges her batteries and opens all channels for her creative juices to flow. These changes in one partner might not be as attractive to the other partner as he might not be ready to undergo any new changes. This can be a threat to the relationship itself if both don't adjust. I can't stress enough how important it is to understand your changing partner at this point because she needs your understanding more than any other time. Talking it out is vital to the changes to come otherwise we can only end up in a closed up situation.

Expressing feelings can be a paralysing challenge for most of us. We dare not admit our feelings to someone else because they may think we are weak so we should bottle it up inside us. Fear of rejection or fear of being judged can stop most of us from admitting our love for our special someone. We must learn to let our emotions flow because holding emotions in the long run can be an exhausting and time wasting activity which will be a liability for our emotions. Acknowledge and accept the love that is given to you with grace and an open heart. In return give your partner abundance in unconditional love and the beauty of your love will reflect and radiate in all aspect of your life. Being in love with a deep, gentle, sensual and nurturing lover is one of the most blissful experiences we will encounter in our lives and hopefully that is the kind of relationship you have. When we learn to let go of anger and resentment and embrace love with gratitude we open our consciousness to the deeper meaning of love. Stop trying to change other people and change the one person you can change that is yourself, this is one hard lesson I had to learn in life before I moved on. When we begin the journey of patiently listening and opening ourselves to change we allow miracles and surprises to walk into our lives. Leave the door open to the world of communication in order to experience a new way of loving. If this kind of love is not shared in your marriage your spiritual journey will not hold you in your present relationship for much longer. It is in silence you finally realize that the relationship is no longer able to sustain because a complete direction must be taken for a relationship that serves no purpose and only you will know when to end a relationship. Being in love is a challenge to ourselves so we must leave our hearts open. We must learn to trust ourselves first in order to trust someone else and you know the meaning of being safe just by trusting yourself first. When you've learned the art of trust you feel comfortable with an intense relationship with the right person because we choose our partners to our highest potential. We have learned to shut down our body to the slightest conflict which we should be aware that conflict open our self love and does not allow us to battle our ego. Unconditional love comes through our spiritual awareness which not all humanity will embrace in their life time. Learn to have faith because faith is the miracle blessing to bringing us closer to our dreams. We can encourage faith by patiently listening to our inner self and letting our little voice speak.

If you want to sort out your problems, let go of your inhibitions and express yourself in hundreds of ways until you make your point across and also worth looking within your own physiological contributions that may be affecting the outlook of your marriage problems. Reveal and get in touch with your true feelings. Sit down and talk to yourself and try to identify what is really bugging you and get working on it. Ask yourself why you feel there is a problem, how you feel about it and what you can do to sort it out in order to sort out yourself and contribute towards sorting out your marriage. Express your feelings and problems to your partner and focus fully to getting your marriage back on track. I am no phycologist and not in any position to advice people of how and why you should stay married or if you should divorce but I give my personalised experience and opinion to use to your advantage, if you wish. Sometimes the soul searching you do will bring your marriage to a down hill because you finally open your eyes to seeing the problems present the way they are and not in the deluded way you used to see them. For me when I realised that I was hiding behind a marriage that does not offer me what is my birth right I had to openly acknowledge what is already quite obvious and what has been for a while even though I was not ready to accept my circumstances. I believed my husband and I were both in denial about the problems we had in our marriage and tried to work on them with no hope and my husband still to this date thinks divorce is not the best option. I tell him that he will thank me one day when he finds a more suited partner to him than I am, a partner that he can call his own spiritual partner because I don't think I am that person and he is not that person to me. The gap between us is too deep and far apart to come to any resolution at this stage of our relationship and I have drifted apart in the process. A relationship that I once thought was right for me is not right anymore and it has become a relationship that stops me from my growth and potential spiritual life.

A divorce or separation is not ever easy but you cannot live in denial you just come to a point and say enough is enough and I should now embrace reality. In my case I wanted a divorce because I was not happy of who I became and how much I have changed from who I was. Over the years I made changes to fit in to my environment and people around me even though the person I was becoming was not the person I would ever be happy with. Then again you don't really see if you are right or wrong to change to be a particular person until the right time comes and you totally focus on being accepted by society. The more I changed to please others, the more I realized I was getting sick of the same old patterns of my partner and my mother in law who I could never make happy and in the process no one could make me happy because I was getting lost of my real personality and focus. I felt stuck and found I could not move forward as my environment was restrictive or controlling and this drove me mad and angry. In laws had a major controlling effect on our relationship from the very start and I found I had no power within our own relationship to make changes we needed to make. My husband and I were moving in different directions, my husband was less attentive and more focused on monitory gains and our love was slowly dying. We sometimes live in a fantasy world that our marriage will survive for ever. Well forever is a very big and long word which I soon came to realize. I cried for help from my husband but he somehow never took me seriously or took notice of me. He probably thought I am his wife and I will always be there no matter what happens. Over time I felt lonely, empty and something missing in my life and I hid myself behind my children, giving and receiving love to my children but eventually that was not satisfying enough for me in the long run. My inner voice was calling out for a pure kind of love, a simple love and a love I can be myself but I did not have it and I was immensely depressed. I told my husband my feelings but be complained that I was nagging him, or I was ungrateful or he was too good for me and I should have an abusive partner like my ex or I was too spoiled and I was treated like a princess and I should be happy with what I have. At first I believe that he was right and I should be lucky to have what I have but eventually his attitude became irritating and all this nonsense became too boring and too tiresome for me and I wanted to escape and run as fast as I could but I couldn't because of my children. I felt I was taken for granted by his family and him but I stood with him like a good wife. One day I realized that this was the end of my marriage because miraculously something erupted like a volcano inside me and miracles started to happen in my life. I finally realized that I was emotionally a prisoner in my marriage and I started to realize how unhappy, empty I was and what I was missing and all the things I sub-consciously wanted. I decided to dedicate some time to think about it and left it at that. Over time I realized that my picture in my sub-conscious of the love and happy family I had did not tally with the love and happiness I now have that made me more determined to end this marriage and not to pretend to be happy when I was not. Meditation became a habit everyday and I asked for guidance and surrendered to the unknown magical powers of this universe to guild me to my birth right to be happy and promised to oblige in the universal path for my own betterment. I realized that this marriage was not for me and that was the new beginning for me and from that day onwards there was no turning back. I made up my mind and took note of my decision to stand by myself and be reliable to myself. I kept my promise to me and stopped listening to all other voices other than my inner voice. I was on a mission to get my life, independence, identity, love, respect and freedom back and I was never going to give away my power to any one ever again. I was tossed and turned by his mother and I put up with all her manipulations and this made me into a very angry person. One day I realized that anger was not healthy for me and I was never an angry person before, so I told my husband that his mother is hurting and insulting me too much and I want to keep my distance from her until I gain my confidence to fight back. When she came to see my boys I kept away from her and talked very little and overtime I started to heal and it has been the best thing for me as well as the family. Where as before I was talking away and arguing but my mother in law is not the kind of woman who listens to sense or details. I soon realized that discussions, apologies or negotiations I had with my mother in law was a waste of time and energy because she made up her own mind to control our lives anyway. All the talks would go to waste and she would do as she wanted. I always felt wasted and hopeless after every discussion I had with her. All the talking did not resolve anything with my mother in law; she just came back stronger each time and her mission was to control me and insult me in order to belittle me. I took all these abuse because of the deep-rooted beliefs of unworthiness which was still lingering around from my previous abusive relationship. I had to teach myself the new kind of respect and to teach myself to love me for who I am and I had to learn to forgive not just my partner but also my previous partner for his abuse. I learned fast to replace negative beliefs with feelings of love and approval and I took drastic measure to make my point across. Our marriage slowly collapsed and the realization that I forgot to live for the moment was apparent to me more now than ever. The time was perfect for this miraculous awakening in my life that I will live for now and go with the flow and not worry about tomorrow or forever. I am not saying that there aren't any marriages which are not for ever because there are couples who work hard to keep their relationship together. When we all get married these magical words of love, commitment and passion flourish each other but only a very few of us remember these very things we fell in love with. When the problems start coming love just happens to run through the back door and that is why there are so many divorces in the world. We forget the chase of our love and we forget in time the magic of love and fall into the pattern of routine. We stop surprising our partner and working his heart muscle in order that it jumps in excitement. We get too caught up in surviving day to day life that we forget to save our marriage. We don't really start a marriage to have a divorce but circumstances do not always permit us the happy ever after. We can deny, plead, beg, bargain, cry and scream all we want but the fact remains that unless the problems are ironed out they will still be lingering around. Even when we file for divorce sometimes we have doubts whether this is the right thing to do and we have to make a choice whether to fix the problem if it is possible or divorce and release the person and allow both to be free. Divorce is the only way sometimes we can salvage ourselves and hold on to our dignity, sanity and self.

Society can look very critically on the person asking out of the marriage, all the while the other partner ended the marriage in every way long before the divorce took place and the marriage was just binding by the marriage certificate. People look at the person who asked for the divorce as the home wrecker without thinking of the problems behind the situation. The community should be respectful of other people's decision and not be too judgmental in areas that they don't understand all facts. The pain of a divorce is immense. You can be grieving and in denial for a long period of time and all the changes you bring to the marriage seem to be a waste of energy causing more pain and anxieties. Partners might want to change as soon as they hear the word separation or divorce but no one can really change unless they have that burning desire to change for the better. People temporarily change for the eye or the show and in actual fact suppress themselves for gains for the moment which will never last because that suppression will want to emerge into an expression sooner or later and the old self will emerge once again. If you tried a marriage or relationship for 11 years like I did and it did not work despite all the help you asked from your partner for a different path and it never happened there is no reason to believe that this marriage can survive in 3 or 12 months. This is what happened to me and while writing this book, which is my journey to my healing I also decided that I must divorce because the marriage was not progressing and has come to a standstill. One third of our marriage problems came from inception of our relationship from my mother in law and then the other one third started progressing from my husband and then I contributed to the rest of the one third and pushed it to the end. When I started contributing to our marriage which was holding on an empty shell, I have had enough and just wanted to push myself in the opposite direction. I did not see any progress in our marriage for the better and it was boring and un-amusing. We both contributed to the problems in our marriage and finally I did not want to sort out our relationship any more because there was too much water under the bridge and I could not get my heart to love my husband the way he deserved to be loved. I have tried, battled and kept it together for 11 years not just with my husband but battled with my mother in law too and was getting sick of it, bored, tired and miserable of the battles I fought on my own which never came to an end. My spiritual journey started around this time and I saw the peaceful light at the end of the tunnel and wanted to head that way. The more I headed for peace and contentment the more I saw what I was missing by living in a pretentious world where there is no place or identity for me. I fought with my mother in law all those years to gain a place in the family and realized I never will gain a place because I was not considered part of that family nor was my children. My children were treated different to the other grand children in the family and there were certain patterns that were hard to be broken with my in-laws. The whole process became a tiresome and loosing battle and found no escape other than for me to shift myself from this environment before I end up to be a person I am not. I already started becoming someone I am not, a victim, a person who was always loosing her patience and could not find a happy environment with her in laws. I finally decided if nothing works then I should release my husband and liberate myself in the process and get out of the marriage as early as possible. I felt that these problems were too deep to go away and if I don't handle them now then I will have to handle them at a later date. I know the way I tried to change myself in order to keep my marriage and I compromised my self, my beliefs, integrity and self esteem and it seem to work for a while until I lost myself totally and started feeling miserable because I did not relate to the person I have become. I questioned why and figured out that I am not me any more. I always wanted his approval and that was a childhood trauma that I had to overcome and I always looked for older men as my partner in order to meet this need and to replace as a father figure, the father I never had because my father died when I was 2 ½ years old. I definitely had issues that I had to sort out and I was determined to sort them out now. My husband anyway complained that I was too clean, too controlling, too fussy, too tidy, too talkative, too demanding, too structured, too routine, too ridged, too boring etc. I tried to ignore all that and gave it a try and the fact is I changed to someone I am not because the type of men I attracted was too comfortable in their own ways that they did not have a need to adapt to a changing world and did not want to understand where I was coming from. My husband loved all my qualities when I thought those qualities to our children and raved on about what a fantastic mother I am and how well the kids behave but these same qualities were not accepted in me. My first partner was verbally abusive and too violent and hit me like a base ball and abused me to the point I did not know who I was and lost my confidence and inner child. Until one day I woke up to realizing this and took measures to leave him and finally left that relationship and moved on and I got over it and became a strong individual. Then fell in love again with my current partner who is not physically violent but verbally bullying and controlling. I probably attracted verbally abusive or bullying men because I had a verbally abusive father a father who was the nicest guy when he wants to be and then very verbally abusive on other occasions and I saw the pattern with my father and my men in my life. I had to forgive my father and release him from my sub conscious mind and then forgive myself and my past and love and accept myself. I soon realized not to give up my wants, needs, dream, aspirations, hopes or my soul to make a marriage work. I have to first work on my own foundations and break these inherited emotional barriers within me before I look to any one else. So this is my spiritual journey in search of my answers to my life questions. I could not find any answers with my mother because she was the type who kept quiet and was happy to be abused for the sake of her family but I was determined I was not going to be that woman in this society and I would change for me and for my children. I did not want my children attracting the same kind of partners in their lives like his parents.

A marriage should be able to be sustained within your dreams and work towards achieving each others dreams and find common goals together. When you have so many unhealthy patterns established, a marriage could never work out. There will always be someone else for both partners who will make a more fulfilling relationship and it is best to let each other go than to live in a bad marriage or bad circumstances because the starting point was all wrong. I never felt comfortable enough with both my partners to talk openly, either I was not comfortable with myself to open up or did not feel I can open up fully to my partners because they were judgemental and they would use my past to attack and hurt me in arguments. I felt very lonely among them and never complete as if there was a piece of me missing which I could never pin point. I felt lost and unable to find my path and lived like this for years.

This book truly has been my spiritual and emotional growth and my healer. Typing these words and understanding what I have researched all these months and the emotions that flows out has been such a console to me especially to understand me more than I have understood me before. This whole process has helped me make life decisions I would not have made other wise. It's opened my mind and my heart to change, the changes that are so needed in my life. Unfortunately I wanted to get out of the marriage even though my husband wanted to change and work on our marriage. I gathered a relationship that we have worked over 10 years and a marriage we have worked over 6 years has gone through enough change and we have come to a standstill where we are pulling in different directions. I am pulling towards a simpler, spiritual life where I want to find peace and he is pulling towards a more extravagant, materialistic life where money will buy everything. I also gathered he was never happy with the request that he be faithful to me after our engagement. He was a play boy before he met me and was never really ready to give up that part of his life but never wanted to give up me either. In demanding that he be faithful to me, he just forced himself to accept it and suppressed himself. Over the years that suppression made him depressed to be tied to one partner and he became annoyed and resented me for taking his freedom which is how he saw the commitment he made to me. When he wanted to change to make our marriage work, I did not want him suppressing himself again because there would be some other factor that comes out in himself for these changes in a later stage in the future. He wanted people to come and go as he pleases in his life and I should not restrict him in this manner and I regret now for restricting him all those years ago. I did not know any better and I now know and it still is not too late as I can release him to be who he wants to be. It has thought me a lesson in relationships that I cannot force someone to do something that they are not ready to do, if they do not willingly accept to choose what they must be in that relationship then I should walk away earlier than make the mistakes later. I will keep this lesson in my heart forever and pursue partners who are in par with my beliefs and who are not giving up their dreams or suppressing themselves for me. I also realised that separation will never recapture what we once had and we could never go back to how things were before. Our relationship and the dynamics have changed. I have learned to love and accept me and understood what my real needs and wants are which were not being fulfilled from my marriage and thereby this marriage can never be sustained to accommodate one person's needs and not the others. What we avoid to take care and repair will knock on our door sooner or later whether it be 5 or 30 years. When you do separate because you have thought about it a lot and tried to work it out, don't ever beg for your partner to come back and compromise yourself. Always remember that you deserve the best and not the left over or second best and do not have to put up with an unhappy marriage. You deserve a great marriage with someone who will deserve you, who will treat you with love and respect and who will take an interest in you personally. When you divorce don't look for a partner to fill the gap just heal your emotions, body and soul.

Go through the pain, loneliness and give yourself the attention you need to heal and welcome the mysteries of life and you will see the positive changes that come your way. Be angry, depressed, and anxious and all the emotions you want to be in a healthy way so you do not hold them inside you. Don't feel you have to rush to heal, take your own time from within and cry your sorrows away, avoid suppressing and holding your emotions. Don't heal to other people's wants, spend time in silence looking within you, meditate and become whole again and invite your inner child into your life and learn to see the world again as a child and an inventor and time will make you reborn again.

Life brings challenges but we are never meant to live in misery, it is not healthy for our soul. If your hard work to save a marriage does not work, let go and embrace the sweet and sour changes that come into your life. We were never expected to live like lost soul's, we are here in this planet and this life time to push ourselves forward though our challenges to better ourselves everyday and achieve in everything we do and thrive. If your marriage did not offer you what you were looking for, move on and learn how to become whole. Make changes within you and learn to bring happiness to yourself. Once you make the changes in yourself and grow as a person all sort of possibilities and changes take place around you. This spiritual awakening and this mystical love is what changed my marriage for ever. The common grounds I once had with my partner disappeared and US became ME and the foundations were unstable to stand on and I was miserably unhappy in my marriage. I truly could not be happy with anything that my marriage offered because I was not myself anymore and was looking to escape and hide. I wanted to run as fast as I could so I can get away from the predicament I was in. I did not have this strong desire to work on my marriage and save its future anymore. I just wanted to go into silence and scrutinise myself and change myself to the highest of my own potential. Changes I personally went through were not the best for my marriage because the problems I was covering up for years came to the surface to face me and our marriage ended. There was no more room in my life for slavery, victimisation, compromising my needs for the sake of my partner and his family, not giving the credit I deserve and acknowledging myself. I came to the point where I have put everyone above me and I have become the care taker of my family without getting anything in return and all that just had to stop. I have become my mother in other words because this is what I saw my mother do all her life. I needed to change, to liberate myself, to break free of all my bad and inherited habits, to lift all restrictions I have placed on myself, to love myself unconditionally, to give myself a proper place in the family without accepting second best, to acknowledge I deserve the best and to know that I have rights to express myself as much as others. I was on a mission to find my souls purpose and step into the path of my spirituality which is very essential for my existence and cannot be put off any more. I had to learn to rely on myself and not let myself down and to let me know that I am a person with values, morals and standards of my own and do not have to try to fit into others peoples belief system and remind myself that I do not need anyone's approval. When I started to achieve my ultimate goal which is to have a strong, peaceful, reliable and working mind and evaluated my marriage at this point, I saw all the faults of both of us and I saw the interference from my mother in law and how much damage has happened. At this point my first reaction was to sigh in disbelief and I left it that way for a few months to consider my options carefully. Slowly, I evaluate our spiritual purpose at this point in our lives because we were brought together for a purpose and may be this is my purpose to learn to rely on my own self to be happy and liberate myself of any attachments with people or things to let my soul live free. I know I had to learn to rely on myself and learn to be strong and stand up for myself and I had to learn to say no because that was a big problem for me all my life. I finally have come to the realisation that I do not have to have all the material things in order to feel fulfilled. All I want was simplicity and pure love to be whole and spiritual. I have come to learn the simple things in life to give without expecting anything in return, to enjoy what I've got in the present moment and have no attachment or great expectations in the future. Live in the present and enjoy the little things in life that bring so much joy. I have learned to love without expecting and love with my free will. My dreams and aspirations are simple as making other people happy and helping them find peace and happiness through simple things in life like children and I want to make sure that these things I want is bringing great joy to the people I love and the world around me. I want to keep learning to know and fulfil my purpose in life and I will be rewarded with the simple things that make me whole in life like love and contentment in this life. My main purpose in life now is to teach what I've come to realise to my children so they can understand and enjoy the benefits of simplicity and the universal law and to contribute my share to make their life a little bit better. I feel it is my commitment and duty to pass my knowledge and in the process keep learning from life.

We see every day that more than 50% of marriages end in divorce and some of them have only lived a short married life. In this day and age the relationships seem to be so fragile and shallow and no deep meaning of who we really are. We are more and more getting confused with so many things in this world that we do not have time to understand the real identity of ourselves and then we try to find this undying happiness from this other person who comes into our lives. In the past, marriages were simply held together for family, social or some other pressure but now we are in an age of technology and information dominated era and we can choose the paths we need to take without the external pressure of pleasing a third party. Why can't we do the same thing and avoid all those third party interference to really learn our true selves. I believe it is a necessity for all couples to attend some form of retreat where they go to a place for a few days or a week to spend in silence, meditation and pray in order to get in touch with the true self. .

We may not talk about the reasons that drive us to divorce or separation but one of the major factors would be our sexual relationship with our partner. Whether we want to accept or not we are designed to attract a mate to create a safe environment to create offspring in order to spread our genes and in order to do this we select the most compatible mate so we fall in love, create a safe home to conceive a child and once this nesting is safe we are ready to repeat the process all over again with the same or another lover. We don't do this intentionally but this is how we are programmed and this is how we multiply. We females attract handsome men and men in turn attract females who are fertile and genetically desirable. So once the nesting is secured and the little baby is born and the female's priority shifts from your mate to the baby to nurture her and protect her which in turn she becomes less sexually active. The initial bond we had by falling in love through the release of oxytocin to enjoy and get excited in sexual encountered is now diminished and the female maintains a high prolactin level for breastfeeding. So sex now becomes undesirable and this leads to emotional instability as sex is a major part of our being. When the oxytocin slowly fades we slowly fall out of love and become hard to maintain an exciting sex life as this spark is no more there. Our relationships are 50% feelings and if we don't have the feelings it is very hard to feel anything. Now that this exiting period has diminished we start seeing all the faults of our partner that we did not see before because we were so blindly in love and all we saw, we did not have any negatives in our subconscious mind. We start to feel these negative emotions such as resentment, frustration, blaming each other, irritability, nagging and we in our deeper mind find no solution than to run away from these negative feeling and liberate ourselves therefore the answer is to separate and divorce. Most of us do not want to have sex without the desire, the need, passion, excitement and animal hunger and instinct. So we withdraw from sexual encounters with our partner because we have just stopped feeling. Chemistry and magnetism are what attract us to people? These changes have altered our needs to a different level. Knowing ourself makes us aware of the new wants and desires of our life and we put out the warrant in search of these qualities that are important to us. This is what keeps burning a person's fire "the hunger, the chase, cravings and the challenge for change to the better and more excitement". We all start our relationship with these qualities but we tend to forget very conveniently. We fall into a routine that predicts exactly what happens to our relationship in order to get a sense of belongingness as we all like to feel secure with knowing we belong somewhere. When the chase stopes we start to feel bored because the excitement is in the chase and we have over the years forgotten the art of hunting and the feelings have turned into bored and lethargic habits. We forget the excitement, surprises and the impulsiveness that love brings into our life. A mother would be so consumed with her children and abandon her husband and the husband might feel she is a good mother and standby her. So unconsciously we have chosen our roles in the relationship without any thought of it and learned to be friends, brother and sister or slaves for our children. This may go on for years and then it turns into a habit which is implanted in our subconscious and a habit hard to break. Over time we have seen this man and woman over and over again and you get bored not that you don't love your partner but you loose that interest in the excitement you used to have. Our brain needs impulsive behaviours from time to time, things that come out of the blue and that was not planned because we are creatures who need stimulation. This is why we humans love to fall in love, take drugs, smoke, drink and do all the things that give your brain stimulation.

I went through so much soul searching that I even started asking if a marriage should be so conventional as most people live it. Can problems really be sorted out without trying to be so realistic and can we think unconventionally which may really spice up our marriage? The man is a hunter and always has been the hunter. If he is hunted, he will eventually rebel and want to go hunting again which is what happened to my husband. This concept of partner sharing is for both male and females but it in my opinion that it works more for men because I do not like to have more than one sexual partner at a time. The concept depends entirely on the individual. Everyone might not agree with me on this subject and I too learned to believe there can be unconventional marriages and after all it is an accepted concept from inception of time. I personally don't like the idea but I know from my husband that it is something he has always wanted and was suppressed due to making a commitment to just one partner. Some of our problems arouse due to diminished quantity of sexual partners in my husbands life which was all so new to him. I did not understand this concept when I got married and do understand now that you cannot stop people from doing what they really want to do. Eventually we all know what we want because our most desired emotions do come to the surface. My husband resented me for taking his freedom which he associated with multiple sexual partners which has been his life style. He never associate sexual contact as a spiritual encounter, it was purely a physical act which did not attach feelings. He always said that he can have numerous partners and not get emotionally attached but I will be his special woman who he will really enjoy sexuality because he has feelings for me. In his words he likes to have appetizers from many restaurants but would like to come to me for the main meal. Most people anyway have affairs behind closed doors and hide the truth from the world out of shame, fear or rejection from society. Fair enough the family truth is not for the entire world to share but can we make this concept a universally accepted fact instead of something to be shamed or criticised about and this is something I still debate with myself. I have accepted the fact that my husband is free to go about his sexuality the way he chooses to but I have decided not to be part of that parade as I value one on one encounters and cannot lower myself to that standard where there is no respect given to me as a person. Obviously we are not spiritual partners and we have served our purpose and now moving on. I just wish my husband luck in his endeavours and thank him and give him gratitude to opening my mind to different concept of life.

I have come to accept marriage as an un-conventional way of living where I will live without expecting, restricting and slowing someone down because of love that is shared between two people. I believe we should have the freedom to choose what we do and a certain amount of freedom to do what we want to do without logging in and out of our partners life. I cannot however share my partner sexually because my body is my temple and I invite people who will respect me as a person and the rest should stay outside that respectable zone. I have no problems accepting other couples do this and I know this happens in the world and try to explore different ways of connecting to try and get that spark back.

This is the time that partners may start joining swing clubs or try different sexual positions or totally open up to a new and exiting partner. Maintain a strong production of sex hormones and can only be maintained with sexual feelings. We want to develop feelings of passion and loving close relationships with our sexual partners and develop inner feelings once again. People these days are in a rush to finish everything and sex has fallen into that same quick and go category. We have no idea how to avoid an orgasm and learn to explore and spend time caressing and slow controlled movement during intercourse with our partner which releases a stream of sexual energy that converts into strong feelings of love and joy. This should be more caressing hand touches and general pleasing sensations and not actual penetration. Use imagination to feel the love you once had and to create it back into the relationship. Just touching, kissing and falling asleep in each others arms skin to skin creates a strong bond in the relationship. We have to stop being selfish thinking about our own sexual pleasures, start thinking of pleasing your partner. Don't think of the ultimate orgasm, just take your time to explore your partner and make her happy and satisfied and in return she will give you the same satisfaction and the ultimate result will be so much greater. Just use your senses to feel the most pleasure of each other and to nourish your lover. You will feel at peace and glow with satisfaction. Just exploring our partner with our hands will release heat and tingles in our body which is the bio-energy that can be experienced by many sensitive individuals. Skin is a highly stimulating organ and can have enormous pleasure with just touch and feelings. Pleasure comes in the preparation in chasing, foreplay, kissing and caressing and get to know your partner and admiring and lying next to her and then start love making. Today accepted format of sex is to have as many partners as possible and it is always just a start where there is no middle and an end. How can we possibly know what real love is when we don't give enough time and effort to one partner to know them inside and out and in return get help to know ourselves. We have an obligation to take time to explore our partner, to just look into her eyes and get to know her for who she really is. When we change partners like we change our clothes we loose touch and fall into more confusion than what is worth and no wonder so many youngsters are confused about sex and love these days. I find this to be one of the major problems in relationships. How wonderful it is to love someone so purely and so unconditionally without expecting anything back. Our health relies on the strong energy level in our body. The connection you make in this form of love making will last for days compared to the quick forms of love making in the modern world. You can connect to your partner in a more higher level than just sex and days that you do not love make just lying next to each other skin to skin will make your bond more stronger. Love making should never be about a quick orgasm, it should always be about bonding with your partner and taking your time to make that bond and connection and to really know her and please her and this is the only form of love making that can sustain a relationship in the long run. The quick sex and orgasm will soon become a bore which will not satisfy a person mentally therefore the person will not be fulfilled and look for another partner and the cycle go on. Hindu's are thought these techniques and they choose a position that is relaxed and they only concentrate on what they are doing with their partners and they follow their sensations, touch and partners. No saliva, oil or lubricant should be used as the time taken to connect with your partner will naturally lubricate the woman and external lubricants will interfere with the sexual energy flow to each other. Sex chakra is our strongest bio energy generator and keeps the sex hormones going. If we block this flow of energy or make it weak we can be as good as sick or old at the same time balance is the key and you don't want to burn from both ends. Improper use of this energy would result to hormonal imbalance and low energy levels. Man may have sex with numerous partners and numerous times but to connect to this one spiritual person and to enjoy and receive total satisfaction through sexual healing is the most beneficial form of love making we can experience. Use and release of proper sexual energy will lead to a more creative, pleasurable, harmonious, peaceful, balanced and happy life. On the other hand over use of improper sexual act or sexual blockages can lead to numerous health problems such as hormonal imbalances, emotional imbalance, depression, food deficiencies, unstable mind etc. Too much masturbation in males could cause deficiency in Zinc and other nutrient loss of the body and too much clitoral stimulation in a woman could make her body tense and make her unaware of true virginal pleasure in order to release true sexual energy. While masturbation is very strenuous to the body the sexual contact in the proper and relaxed manner with the opposite sex can bring a calming, peaceful, content and happy effect to us. Improper use of sex causes hormonal imbalance and this hormonal imbalance could have drastic effect on addictive behaviours such as alcohol abuse, drug abuse, behaviour problems, gambling, aggression and violence. Woman would build emotional problems, nervous problems or totally loose sexual appetite and men will be less emotional, develop heart disease, prostate problems or impotence in the long run. That skin to skin touch, foreplay, taking time to know and connect your partner is becoming history in our society more and more. It has become a game of numbers and the thrill for young people to have the highest amount of sexual partners to boast about. How many of those partners did you really enjoy sexual contact with in the first place, I bet just a hand full, so was it worth it, may be just to tell your friend how many sexual partners you have had might be the only benefit. We must all be educated in the perfect formula for Love, sex, Health, contentment and happiness is to hug, touch, kiss, feel, massage, whisper sweet nothings, patients, take your time and love your partner with your whole self and like you would love your own self. Experience the moment and the ecstasy and you will be rewarded with the fulfilment of what is the highest form experience in this life. Have you notice how much a little baby needs touch and love and when showered with love he will wiggle with radiance and excitement in his own way and stop crying and snuggle into the cuddles and love that is showered upon him. Do you know the best thing for a baby as soon as he is born is to have skin to skin contact with his mother and breastfeed within the first hour of birth? The mother and baby benefits long lasting emotional healing and bond due to the physical and skin contact and they both thrive. Have you seen the pleasure a baby gets from suckling into his mothers breast the most form of pleasure a baby gets is through sucking and the skin contact with his mother makes it more pleasurable to him and calms him down instantly. When a mother and baby are separated for a longer period of time after birth the emotional trauma for the mother and baby are great. The baby and mother need constant contact with each other and the mother needs to breastfeed and nurture her child. We as adults have not changed that much, the child in us is still there and we have to learn to connect to this with our partner in the form of touch and sensuality to connect to that childlikeness in ourselves. So reconnect the child in you with the help of your partner and help him connect in the process. Skin contact is more important to human functioning than we care to admit. Do not be afraid to admit that you need love and sensuality and touch for you to thrive as a person I know I do.

Emotional and sexual problems start at the time of birth if mother and baby are separated for a long period of time and does not allow that skin to skin bonding process and if the baby is bottle fed and not breast feed. The mother's breast should be the primary and first choice of feeding the child and emotional satisfaction for her baby. All bottles, dummies, thumbs should be eliminated as much as possible and should be replaced with the mothers breast for as long and as often as the baby has a need to suckle. Emotionally deprived children will have violence, anger, aggression, criminal, destructive, shyness, lack of confidence and lot more other problems in their adulthood. Children should be shown love, caressed, hugged, kissed and payed attention to in their childhood in order that they grow into emotionally balance individuals. Parents can help the child of the opposite sex to over come autism, violence, ADD and hyperactivity through their physical contact, closeness, touch, hugging and kissing. Only through being loving with our partners can we be a good example to all these lessons we should teach our kids. If all couples learn the art of loving deep within, our world will radiate with this spiritual kind of love and help our future generation in the process. I want all of us to know we can start creating the love this world needs in the comfort of our own bed room and in the comfort of our own loving partner. I don't see why we can't all contribute to starting our love generators in this simplest form and start radiating that love into your children and then to the world.

CHAPTER 7

Letting Your Partner Free And Liberating Yourself

Think about the relationships, ideas, attitudes, belongings, commitments, dreams, habits and obligations we have, do they suit us now and bring the contentment and joy it did at one particular time of your life. If not it is time to let go. Take stock of your baggage in all parts of your life and streamline them and decide what should let go and what should stay because we really don't need everything we have, it has just become a habit to have it. We should every now and then empty our garbage bins in any area of our life. Time will always tell us which commitments, relationships, desires, values, needs and things would serve us better and which should go. It is important for the natural selection to take place and let what is worth to be held and what is not to be released. While writing this book, I have come to realise that my marriage was blocking my creativity and we were both suppressing each other. Our marriage served no purpose to either of us any more and was becoming a hindrance. Now it was time to let it go of our marriage and each other. One of the most important lessons I've learned is not to wait for others to change to the way I want them to change, instead just change and grow myself as a person and find the peace and happiness within me. I now enjoy the people around me when they are there and if that relationship does not serve a purpose in the future then I will look at it at that point and release it because holding on is not the way for me to live any more. It impossible to change some one else until that person wants to change. The changes you make will lead you to contentment within yourself and that is the greatest form of wealth you will find in this world. To not have any attachment to people or things will be the most rewarding achievement you will accomplish. Listen to your inner self, your subconscious mind and what your inner child is trying to say. Listen to the silence as silence will bring all the answers you need in your life. When you let go of things and even let go of people who you love, you are allowing the freedom for things to come and go freely and this nonattachment may sound cold but this is the only way to free and liberate ourselves, to create less complications in our lives, to reach above to our higher conscious mind and the way to ask for guidance to better our lives and our spirit. Unconditional love is to love someone so purely and so intensely that nothing will stop you loving him even if he does not return your love. If he returns your love that would be wonderful but you cannot tell someone how and when to love so if you get love returned that is great and if not and if you really love someone you will love him regardless of what you get in return because true love has no attachments or conditions.

I don't believe in being stuck in an unhappy marriage and I think the philosophies of marriage are rapidly changing in our society. Most times trying to hide behind a bad marriage hinders our spiritual growth because we are so miserably unhappy in that marriage and our brains stop functioning. A marriage is what the partners in the marriage want it to be and how ever long they would like to live in that partnership. Our human brains naturally have an animal instinct build in which makes us not want to be restricted. The restrictions placed will one day want to come to the surface and rebel. In an ideal world people are free to choose what ever they want to do and be who ever they want to be. In my husbands case the restrictions I placed on him to be a one woman man crumbled his picture perfect dream of his fantasy world to be free with his unlimited maidens. When his dream that he build and had for so long was taken away instantly, his dreams, his attitude, opinions and energy level slowly diminish to a point where he got depressed, stuck, robot like and then slowly got bored with everything. We spoke about this topic many times but instead of releasing him into the wild where he has his free will I did not give him any choice to share and insisted that I will be his only partner if he needs a marriage with me. He was never mentally ready for one woman and he still is not ready for one woman today and I should never have confined him to the small space around me. He probably got bored with my structure, order and organised environment because it was all very predictable in his opinion. Everything in the house had a place and that is where they were always kept and he was not used to this kind of structure where as I was brought up this way in boarding school and I probably put him through hell with my tidiness and organisational skills. He always waited for the red notice to come in to pay his bills and where as I always paid the bills as soon as they came and well before the due date. Your brain knows the current styles and the routine and is bored with the similar way of patterns that work everyday and he probably had enough of this organised boring life. I like structure in life but at the same time like impulse in other areas of my life. You can change the techniques, change the mood, change the style, change your looks, cut your hair or grow your hair, and change the place but most of who we are stays the same. After all our relationships are a lot based on half relationship and half our mental attitude. We need impulse and surprise in order to break habits and routine and we need our heart muscle to start racing and build a sweat. Simply, we human creatures need stimulations and that is why people drink coffee, smoke, drink alcohol, take drugs and do stunts because they need stimulation and we need this kind of excitement even in our sexuality.

Changing partners has been a natural occurrence from inception of time and we these days have numerous partners for all sorts of reasons and it is also natural for some to have more than one partner at a time. We want a new sexual partner in our life when we separate or divorce from our partner. I personally cannot allow myself to be available to two partners at the same time sexually. I believe one partner deserves my undivided attention at all times and if I cannot give that attention to him I should move on before I make myself available to another. I will enjoy my partner as long as I have him and as long as that relationship is healthy and if he chooses to want more than one partner I will happily release him and let him go to find his exploration. If you restrict him, he will want to find out a way for his boredom and try it behind my back anyway. You cannot make someone do something they don't want, you can only accept them the way they are or walk away, which is exactly what I did. The easiest concept is to open our hearts to the new changing world and change the rules and accept your partner for the number of maidens he may have, if that is a concept you can comprehend. It has never been a secret that man always lived a life with more than one woman at a time and it is clearly written even in history books and the bible. After all if a man's desire is to live his animal instinct to his full potential there will be no stopping it. I will never make the mistake of holding a man under my spell ever again if he is not happy to be there on his own free will. I have finally accepted polygamy because it is a fact of most relationships and our society. Polygamy is made easy by lot of societies or clubs in the world such as the swingers clubs where they swap their spouses with others. We all want marriage and family to one partner but our world is full of infidelity which happens everyday with some family or another. So what do we really need, we need this foundation in this one long lasting partner for our security purpose and on the other hand explore our animal urge and seek all our erotic fantasies through a partner purely just for fun. We can pretend that animal ran away to the wild the day we got married but would some of us be kidding ourselves to tame that tiger within ourselves. It all depends on what people are game to explore and experiment and I have heard of people who are very willing to swap and explore other people's partners. We live in a free world to do and choose as we please and if the couple is in agreement then why should any one else question the motives behind that relationship. Personally I feel that we can have our cake and eat it too. I question, why we can't work hard enough to have the security, foundation and also experiment our fantasies and animal instincts with just the one partner. If we speak out our fantasies to each other that would bring about better bonding and communicational skills into the relationship. If we cannot trust and rely on our partner totally with every aspect of our life then we are not living with our soul mate and our spiritual partner and that would be more a question to scrutinise than the sexuality side of it. I would say that this will gain far greater results with abundance in the long run and cement the relationship.

So with all these going on why do we fall in love over and over again despite all the mistakes we make and the heart aches we bear? When we fall in love parts of our brain is linked to feelings of true love and we all know how love makes us feel. We feel over the clouds, we are in a fantasy world and it makes us feel really good. When we are in love we lose our appetite, cannot concentrate, we cannot sleep, feel obsessed with this person, stutter, feel breathless, butterflies in our stomachs. Men are more attracted to beauty, while women are more attracted to money, education and position.

Both men and women are excited by those who are mysterious-probably because Mystery triggers the activity of dopamine in the brain. And both sexes tend to fall in love with those of a similar background and values. We also fall in love with someone who fits within what's called our "Love map." This is an unconscious list of traits we seek in our ideal partner that we build as we grow up. We are unconsciously attracted to those who complement ourselves? We find mating and parenting to ensure the continuation of the human Race. We do not have to analyse why we fall in love, we just need to learn the heavenly enjoyments that mysteries of love bring for fulfilment that makes us feel so complete. To love and be loved so totally is a spiritual experience that the heavens have send us and that does not belong to the energies of this world. Embrace the pure and true soul mate that comes once in your life time and love, learn and grow with this person as the day you meet him your spiritual life starts. I cannot tell you the feelings of love, sensuality, romance, balance and the creativity you feel inside you, you totally get mesmerised by this beauty of love. There certainly is nothing like love in this world. Love makes the world go round and things start to make sense.

I feel today that I don't necessarily have to be married to be with my soul mate. If marriage comes that is fine but if it doesn't then learn to enjoy the moment. Couples can live in and out of marriage and choose how well marriage will suit them. If we marry and find it is wrong, we don't necessarily have to be stuck in a mistake for the rest of our life and shut down our creativity for ever. Releasing of sexual energy will create the lava for creativity and open up our chakra's that were shut and make our juices flow freely. The ultimate sacrifice you do for your lover will bring a marriage closer together because his creative mind would be experiencing those erotic moments in his head and want to please you more and bring you to your highest climax. This I see as the problem solvers for all marriages a break from each other to the unknown and comeback with love and gratefulness to your partners. This new found freedom of togetherness without the barriers of jealousy, hatred but pure love. This will open you as a person without fear to enter new dimensions and explore this big spiritual journey we are here in this world to accomplish. This spiritual journey is huge and everlasting and cannot be entered if we hold ourselves back. Best way to liberate ourselves is to let go and choose to be free and have no boundaries or restrictions. Our soul mate and spiritual partner necessarily does not have to be your marriage partner, it could be someone else and only you will know that answer.

What a great feeling it is to let go and live free and peaceful. Letting your partner free is the noblest thing you can do for another person. Letting go of your partner is not going to be possible if you haven't fully let gone your fears. Fear is one of the most negative factors that we human give away our power to. The fear of the unknown can literally kill us and our soul.

Before you consider the possibility of letting go of your partner take a good look into your self and look at the tendencies of jealousy, fear and unhappiness in your own self. Look at where these feelings came from and how it got stuck in you for such a long time. These feelings could be due to one or more bad relationships you had in your life or may be they are feelings due to negative childhood experiences. Forgive yourself and teach yourself to forgive others and accept and love yourself in the process. Be so grateful for all those relationships and circumstances that thought you along the way and eventually helped you be who you are today. Be so grateful for everyone who came into your life so far as they all helped you in some way or another to be who you are today.

Ten years ago, I was a very possessive woman. I am grateful for my partner and marriage as this relationship brought up all the negative sides of me to the surface in order that I can deal with them appropriately and I worked hard to get myself sorted out and I got over it and I am proud to be who I am today. I have let him free to be him and let him go on his own path without my interference. I healed and accepted me for who I am but these healing brought other feelings to the surface. I started to be and feel strong but I became an angry person over time and I realised that my husband and his mother was always undermining, suppressing and disrespecting me all the time and I did not like these conditions put on me but instead of saying it out loud I started to keep these issues inside me. Over time I became angrier and exploded with emotional trauma and asked my mother in law to keep away from me if she cannot respect me. I distanced her and still found I was angry and realised that it was time to break my marriage so I can start being myself. Today I am separated and in the process of getting a divorce and I feel free as a bird and happy as a song. Forever is a very long word, which consumes too much energy for my liking and I don't want to waste my good energy worrying about it. I want to enjoy the moment now and my future will lead me to where I am supposed to go with all the surprises that are in store for me. I am content with that idea. I am content that I have learned very hard to let go and I have worked on it for so many years and finally found victory in the concept of liberation. I am proud of my hard work and know what enormous effort and courage I had to put through to come to this very moment and my wish is to help all man kind achieve that kind of liberation. To feel free is to liberate and let go of all that you hold dear to you. Letting others free will bring the joy, love, contentment and most of all the trust you lost so long ago or you never had. Try it and you will be pleasantly surprised and how such a simple act takes so much energy to achieve yet when achieved brings so much joy and inner peace. You finally do touch your soul and you can breathe again because unconditional love and spirituality helps you heal.

Many human beings are victim and we are used by others. Don't let others use you and don't use other people either. Do not be a victim to any one or any of your circumstance just takes the challenge and sort out the problem without sitting around feeling sorry for yourself. Live moment to moment in the present. Our suffering comes from like and dislike, also the cause of our problems is lust, greed, attachment, desire, etc. Our feelings will come and go and this restless craving is what drives us to seek fresh amusements from our lives which lead to our sufferings in the present and the future. We want things to be permanent and the only way to liberate our cravings is to let go of these attachments we have and liberate ourselves and live for the moment. If we direct our mind into the proper thoughts and intentions and keep focused with our will power and determinations we can break the barriers of the human addictive behaviours that bring us suffering. Learning to control our mind and thoughts and letting ourselves free is the highest form of liberation there is and in the process we can liberate the people we love in our lives.

Any emotion we do not express will be stuck inside us and make it bigger than it is over time causing so much havoc in our lives. It is imperative that these emotions that are stuck be released and you can get guidance through meditation, silence and asking help from your higher power. Learn the art of forgiveness not just to others but also to yourself. Healing would start with the act of forgiveness as we cannot fully love and accept either us or others until we learn the art of forgiving. Write a list of all people you have the need to forgive, the people who you believe did wrong by you in the past such as parents, in laws, brothers, sisters, ex-husband, children etc. and then write why you should forgive them and for what particular reason. Did they make you disappointed, sad, insecure, fearful, resentment or anger what ever it is go through your reasons and learn to let go and release these into the universe and tell yourself it is OK to forgive yourself and that you are adult enough to understand what the other person was going through and that you release this resentment and forgive for the good of that person and yourself and that you release them from your hold. In your mental picture hug and release this person with your love and keep that picture stuck in your head so you always remember that this person is your friend now and not your enemy and in return you are detoxifying your negative emotions. Finally forgive yourself for all the wrong you have done in your life and the wrong and destructive patterns you have attracted into your life and finally imagine yourself free and flying away like a bird. Just know and feel strongly that this is the first step to liberating yourself and do not do this for anyone else but yourself. You can write a letter to each one of these people and either give it to them, mail it or just burn it. Writing a letter will let all your emotions flow, do not hold anything in, just let it out and put it on paper. Then leave this letter somewhere for a month or so and read it and see what is in that letter and sort out your emotions. You can now send this letter to that person or simply burn it as the healing has already started in your sub conscious mind.

Being overweight is another emotional problem we humans have. Ask yourself if you were abused when you were young or was food used as a reward or are you eating huge amounts of sugar or fatty products to keep you satisfied because you are so bored or unfulfilled in your life. If you have a secure relationship with an understanding partner to talk about your negative feelings this will help to rely on your partner instead of food. If there is so much anger that you really need to be expressed take a pillow go to bed and punch it with all your energy or punch a boxing bag or lock yourself inside the car put the music loud and scream as loud as you can. Just get this anger, resentment and emotions out and you will feel good after this. When you are hitting the pillow make sure you think of the person you resent or angry and hit as hard as you can and tell the pillow why you just punched and what you want sorted out. If you want to talk about someone you trust or a therapist talks about everything that you are bottling up inside yourself. Acknowledge to people that you are not in a good mood or that you are angry and don't be scared to express or talk about your feeling or emotions. Ask people for your space if you feel you need it and look within to heal yourself from inside. Also repressed sexual energy, resentment, bad habits and worry can have an enormous effect on the health and well being of your body and can cause so many diseases if these negative behaviours are not released properly. The only way to overcome these problems are to love yourself without any limitation and with all you have. Some people are so scared to die or to be ill that they do not talk about these topics and avoid these topics at all costs. We have to remember that dying is part of living and should be celebrated as much as birth. Death should be a celebration of the person's life. Dying is as much part of life and living. In order to change misery in your life you should simply change your attitude. Liberation means to be entirely free, free of all attachments.

CHAPTER 8

The Ultimate Spiritual Growth

Spirituality means different things to different people. In stead of trying to comprehend all versions of spirituality, I will just go by what I believe spirituality is for me. Spirituality to me is I can see the world and everyone with absolute beauty and with unconditional love. It is the ecstasy of knowing my true self and to discover the real conscious and unconsciousness of me. To love myself for who I am and for what I am and in return treat other people the way I would like to be treated. In the process of learning myself I would like to teach my findings so others, so they can help themselves be someone happier and live a better life. I like to accept universal laws to the best of my knowledge which in return help me understand people around me better. We should not be ignorant to the fact that our way of thinking is the only correct way of thinking and not give any regard to other people's way of thinking.

It is easy for us to have a false sense of who we are as we have listened to our parents, relatives and teaches of whom they think we are and have never really explored the volcano that is resting deep inside. The individual ego we have is very different to our real identity. When we discover our true self we feel the inner peace, security and happiness that this world cannot usually bring through materialistic wealth. We feel finally free to be ourselves and out of the cage we have lived our whole life. This inner peace could be what some would call knowing God or your higher conscious. I like to think that my higher conscious finds my real journey, the journey I've come to deliver in this life time no matter how happy or painful it may be. I am here with a purpose and my spirituality brings me closer to my objective purpose every single day. When I finally know my true self I will also know my true journey and I will oblige to work in par with the universe to do good to all humanity and in return find my inner peace. To surrender to the light and fulfil my purpose and calling and travel into the depth of the unknown with faith and purpose is the ultimate goal I have. To know yourself is like a higher power inside you with a on off switch that you can turn on at any time. If you are to connect with your higher self you have to learn to connect in a deeper level and feel the inner joy that radiates from you. The trust you build and the trust level you experience with yourself and your inner self should be second to none because your higher self knows what is best for you like no body else. Sit patiently and listen to absolute silence and you will hear if you care to listen, your inner voice talking to you of your life directions and which path to take. Pay close attention to words or signs you may get and ask your higher conscious what they mean if you are not aware because those are the leading signes to your spiritual and future path that must be taken. Respect the answers given and send gratitude to the universe for allowing this harmonious connection between you and your spirit to finally come to some understanding to be comfortable enough to communicate.

Spiritual knowledge is the one thing that destroys our trouble and in the process if we help others with the spiritual knowledge we have attained, we have achieved happiness in the highest form possible. If you are spiritually strong you are strong in every way as spirituality is the only form of goodness for our soul and our soul is the strength to our real self.

Get into the world and learn the secret of the universal law. The more we learn about this secretive power and we start to use it in our everyday life the more I find we stop judging ourself and other people around us. I am a student in this planet to understand how the world works and to learn and study my spiritual journey and who or what gives me the right to judge my family, friend, husband, child or the people around me absolutely nothing. When we start noticing the strength, power, courage, persistence and love growing around us and within you, your world completely changes and you find the new meaning of life and the meaning you live for. You feel how insignificant you are when there are so many causes in the world that needs our help. The whole universe is of perfect balance and that is how nature created it and it is our responsibility as humans to help our fellow man live in harmony. How much money do we need to live our lives and why not share our abundance with the children starving in this world or to give someone in need a better day today than yesterday? Let us only learn to judge people with their greatness and not their imperfections, misfortune or mistakes. We have all been in that cowardly situation to judge another when there is so much more we can better ourselves within. We are all one in this one world and should work as one to achieve some greatness may be not today or tomorrow but that day will come sooner than we think. Our work together as a nation, country and world is the only commitment we must have as a common goal and the vision to see what must be changed not today but NOW. Silence is the way to the truth. Our ultimate spiritual growth is for us is to grow and use our potential mind power to the greater benefit of the world. When the human is ready to move and embrace this infinite power, there are no boundaries or stopping this soul from radiating his magical powers to the world and helping heal the universe.

Our world is moving and our mind, body and spirit are growing and we cannot see this intense process because we don't feel this connection to the earth. When we fine tune into the outer world, our spirituality, our aura and our soul's journey we realize that everything that happens to us is within our control. Every little thought or details are conceived in our sub-conscious mind and we gave power to it to grow. When we are tuned into the electrical vibes that move us with the universe we can see the changes before it happens and we have the power in our brain to make it a reality or stop the process then and there and this is the secret to our soul's journey cause we control everything within our power. We can bring profound perfection and beauty into our lives as when we are in love with the world and the people in it; we cannot see anything else other than perfection and beauty. We see every man handsome and every woman beautiful in their own right and this is the unconditional love we radiate to our fellow man. There is no end to our brain power and we use it and manipulate it to do good to our fellow man and help every person in this world and our power is all in our spirit. Feel your spirit, that is born so free, that does not have any attachment and can move freely from one incarnation to another can you say the same about your body which holds money and possession so dear. Mediate in silence and free yourself of all anxiety and attachment and free yourself to receive the abundance of life to a greater purpose than the material world that is on offer everyday of our lives. We may have everything in our lives but it is just an external game that we fall into to fulfil our egoistic society and to try and fit in. There would be no peace in this kind of living until your soul is free of all attachment to embrace the pure infinite journey that we are born to fulfil for our spiritual growth. When we learn to liberate ourselves this will be the first step to our learning and growing process. Love with unconditional love and live with faith of the power within you and you will find in life what you must in order to fulfil your life's purpose. Meditate and ask for help from your sub conscious and you will get the guidance you need and will be shown the path to your life. Silence and listening to what your inner self say is the best method of getting the answers you need. You can also relax, meditate or do yoga to get the help you need. To know one self, I mean to really know yourself in and out is the highest form of achievement you can achieve in this plane. If you don't know yourself well enough you really know nothing. Perfection is born in every one as her birth right but our ignorance make it a struggle to express. Learn the secret of controlling your life through your mind because this was always yours but we adults forget in the process of growing up.

Sexuality and spirituality has a close connection to each other because both are open to love and both energies can be channelled in positive and creative forms. The positive energy, strength and most of all the love, passion, desire we feel will open our hearts and minds to the world of possibilities and make us feel capable of doing anything we put our minds to. After all we are not capable of knowing our selves sexually if we do not know ourselves enough. When we do get to know our real self we are also aware of ourselves spiritually and sexually which is closely connected. This creative sexual energy can be redirected into achieving miracles in personal growth and professional achievements. Tantric Sex are forms of sexual activities practiced in Hinduism to connect with their partner. Practicing tantric sex brings joyous mind and glimpse of heaven on earth. Visualizing and connecting are the importance of tantric sex. If a couple wants to connect in this spiritual form both should not have sex for a few weeks and have a strong sexual desire in order to make it a pleasurable and spiritually connecting experience. Choose a time near ovulation and when both are in full spirits. Another form of healing is cleansing your seven chakras through meditation and this meditation can be done while love making with your partner for a more bonding and closer encounter. You may light some candles, have some music or an oil lamp to intensify these sensations you feel and become one spiritually and sexually. Focus on your partner's body and the touch of the skin and the love you feel for each other. Our main focus as a man or woman is to get a climax in an orgasm and we forget the whole process because it is just such a fast reunion between two people. In this fast moving world we have forgotten to sit and enjoy the good things in life including our partners and really explore and know the things that matter to her or him. Sexuality can be a new found means of getting to know your partner for the longer run and we can make this into a spiritual and calming process that no disturbances of the world will interfere in this love making process. Our main aim should be to be whole again with our new found love, contentment and our partner and help each other reach this goal together. The satisfaction you get through meditative love making with your other half is a tantalizing and fulfilling feeling and experience that will connect you for a longer period of time than the traditional quick sex act.

You can use sexual energy as a stimulant or an electricity to energise your whole body and use this energy as a will power to connect with what ever it is you want to do or be in life.

At the end of everything all we really want is happiness and contentment in anything we do so we really should not have to suffer any pain. So why does all this go wrong for us and how do we end up in the failures we do? Our mind programming took place long before we even knew ourselves in our childhood. The way our parents treated us, spent time with us and the way they treated each other. We soon enough realised and grasped that this is the way of life and the way of how relationships are formed without even consciously thinking about it just by observing our surrounding. If we were given a happy environment to flourish we are basically given a foundation to form good emotional relationships and it will make it easier to make up our mind and have the will power to a positive relationship with ourselves as well as our partners. But if worry and anger were part of our childhood we will cope more negatively in our adulthood. We were unconsciously our parent's guineapigs to programming negatives in to our brains and as a result what ever we do we end up being unhappy from inside and we have no answers for why these feelings emerge. Our subconscious mind somehow takes over our conscious minds and until we re program our subconscious we will live with these negative that our parents bread in us. Our subconscious mind is made of dreams and the faith and belief system which is the only way to work with our subconscious mind. There is no other easy way out. We have to feel emotionally towards our beliefs and have real meaning to these beliefs we need to adapt to, to change into our new person with the new found emotional, spiritual and mental beings.

Our senses are the way we experience our lives and if you take an infant look at how he would experience his outer world by putting everything in his mouth and really staring at objects that come in front of him and really feeling with his tongue the taste. If you are not capable of feeling you really have no enjoyment in life as feelings are our wheel to this life. Emotional satisfaction makes us happy at the end of the day not the money in the bank account or the cars parked in the garage, it is our emotional satisfaction that guarantees our happiness and how we meet those needs. If we always have the inner child in us we can always connect to the way we feel and always somehow find the solutions and way to happiness. Our inner exploring child will take us with her creative mind to the place where we want to go or be to be happy. It is every parent's duty to be a role model to creating tender loving feelings in our children. It is very important for children to cuddle, kiss and hug the opposite sex parents in order to develop a healthy sexual relationships in the future.

I have come to realise that the reason I have a problem with my relationships are because I never had a father figure in my house hold and never got a chance to hug, kiss or cuddle my father and on the other hand my mother was never a person to hug and was very distant. I grew up craving this kind of love and created the dream in my mind and I am determined to find the kind of love that is best and right for me and I know and feel that I will find it. I have a very loving and close relationship with my boys because I want them to grow up to be very emotionally intelligent men one day and show their emotions to the women that they come across.

Everything mental and physical we learn are discoveries of experiences that leave a mark on us for ever. Get to know people's real person by what they do and for not what they say. You will know a great person when his personality does not change with his achievements in status or monetary gains. The actions we see in a man is a replay of his inner most thoughts and the will power of this man through his persistence. We become responsible for whom we've become as our past has designed and created our present and this present moment will create our future. Learn and work clever in the present moment to make your future moments bright and fulfilling and this will tap into your inner soul and find your spiritual journey.

Knowledge is what keeps life revolving and if you stop learning you are as good as dead. Every idea that you have in the mind has a counterpart in a world, the world and the thought are inseparable. Knowledge is within ourselves Knowledge although the capacity to know is inside us, it must be called out. Working as master of our own mind gives rise to the bliss of non attachment. It is there because the soul must have knowledge, and through knowledge free itself. If a man can do good to others without thinking of himself or the gains he may receive from his doing to others is a very noble man and have attained the highest accomplishment in this life time. The rewards that come to him through his acts of kindness the universe will pay dividends more than his wildest dreams. The man who has lived a rat race life find it hard to stay still and connect to the silence that brings peace and balance. We must all stop and think of the long term peace and contentment that can be brought into our lives which is only through silence and let our inner voice speak. He will learn to control and direct our mind to places we want to go and to control our own destiny the way we have planned in our inner mind. If you constantly sit in silence and allow your inner voice to speak and through the silence he will know the secret to his destiny which is determined will power which only he could control in his own power. We learn over time with persistence to control our selfishness and to work for the betterment of all mankind. Don't judge other people with your standards as they have their own.

Accumulate good Karma as Karma is what we earn through our good and bad doing in this life time and our past life times. Help yourself with a chakra cleanse to open more into the world and the abundant of life. Connect with the infinite power that surrounds us and enjoy the simplicity and the beauty life brings into our lives.

I have given a brief description below of what chakras are as follows:

CHAKRAS

Chakra is the aura or energy that flow in our body. There are 7 Chakras in our body and all our senses, thinking and feelings affect these chakras by opening and closing them. We believe everything is possible to attain and study of chakras allow us to understand our consciousness and how it affects the energy in our body. The seven chakras are

Throat Chakra: This is located at the base of the throat and controls our communication and artistic expression. We should listen to our intuition to guide us to achieving our goals.

Crown Chakra: Located at the top the head and controls awareness or separation with our biological father. When this chakra is closed you feel lonely and find difficult to connect with others.

Brow Chakra: Also called the third eye and located at the centre of the forehead. This is associated with our spirit and spirituality and true motivation to direct our lives.

Heart Chakra: is located at the centre of the chest and controls relationships of spouse, children, parents and everyone you love.

Solar Plexus Chakra: located at the solar plexus and controls power and freedom.

Orange Chakra: located at the centre of the abdomen and controls food and sex. This chakra tells you what your needs, wants and pleasures are. Pregnancy/conception and to be able to feel ones emotions are also controlled by this chakra.

Root Chakra: located between the anus and the sex organs (perineum) and controls trust, relationship with money, survival, security, home, job and to live in the present. This is the chakra to satisfy ones inner being, connection with their mother and how a person feels about the world

Short Biography of Jeanette De Jonk

The father I loved endlessly, died when I was 2 ½ leaving an empty space in my heart. I shed many tears making it my soul's purpose to fill this gap, looking for this perfect father figure in all my relationships putting love at last.

Magically, December 2006 I woke up from a deep seated sleep and was touched by something or someone who pierced through my heart with true love. I saw through all my past traumas and found my true self with this magical love. The bottled up emotions wanted an outlet for expression and the hidden creative juices started to flow forcefully, sparking the steps to enlightenment. I finally heard my inner voice talking to me, the voice that I had safely tucked away. I am totally and blissfully in love with this magic that found my true identity.

The old, the hindrances and people who stood as barriers had to go in order I live in par with my soul's purpose. My marriage, the feeder of fear that blocked me had to be released for my redemption. I have found peace with my soul and the Divine Sources who introduced this magical love to find the balance I so missed. I have always had the will; I just needed to find the way to reach the Divine.

Love will come and go but the imprints of true love I have found will never leave my heart or soul because "love is forever".

www.ingramcontent.com/pod-product-compliance
Ingram Content Group UK Ltd.
Pitfield, Milton Keynes, MK11 3LW, UK
UKHW020135250726
13967UKWH00002B/669